GOD, YOU'RE FIRED

RECONSTRUCTING YOUR LIFE AFTER SUICIDE
LOSS WHILE FINDING HEALING, HOPE AND A
NEW PERSPECTIVE

VICTORIA MYERS

Dear Son,

I thought I understood how deep a mother's love ran, but I didn't —not fully—not until I felt the depth of your loss. I know you're in Heaven, and as your little brother reminded me, "more alive than we are here!" (see 2 Corinthians 5:4). We all love and miss you terribly, but we take heart in knowing you are no longer in pain. For that, we are thankful.

While I live on this earth, I imagine I will forever be sorry I didn't fully understand your sickness and your pain. Though there is nothing I can do about that now, as hard as it is, I must continually lay that heartache down.

I wrote this book to bring honor to you, our son and brother. You were such an amazing and beautiful young man, and you deserve to be remembered and known for so much more than just how your life ended. It was truly an honor to be your mother. And although my days of mothering you here on this earth are done, I will always love you, think of you, and carry you in my heart.

I want you to know I'm going to use your story to save others. I know your heart and how you loved and served others, and I know nothing would make you prouder than to see your family working together to help prevent others from having to go through the silent pain and torment you went through.

This is one thing we can do. One thing we *will* do.

I'm going to use your story to help others see that the major depression that overtook you is *not* a personal failure or weakness but a sickness that can overcome any one of us. I'm going to use your story to bring education and awareness so others may not have to go through the excruciating pain, fear, anxiety, guilt, and a million other emotions that survivors of suicide loss endure.

We're going to make you proud. We are going to take everything Satan meant for our destruction and use it for good.

Meet me at the gate, son. I'll be there as soon as my work here is done.

Love,
Mom

Until We Meet Again

Heather Flood

So short your time
here with us.
It's selfish to want you back,
but we miss you so much.
You lit up the world
with your smile and laughter,
and now you'll watch over us
from heaven, ever after.
You were on your way
to being an amazing man,
but God saw more for you.
He had a greater plan.
We will never forget you.
You'll always live in our heart,
and with you smiling down on us,
we will never part.
One day the tears will stop,
and the hurt we feel may end,
but you will always live on,
son, brother, grandson, friend.
So don't worry.
We will somehow carry on,
finding comfort and peace
that you're in heaven above.
We will always miss you.
We will always want you here,
but there are no good-byes
in the waterfall of tears.
We shall meet once more.
Your smile we will see again,

but you've just started what we all long for,
a life in heaven that has no end.
And though the world is a little darker
without you to light up our days,
we will see your smile forevermore
in the twinkling stars and shining sun's rays.

Until we meet again . . .

CONTENTS

Preface

If you have lost a loved one to suicide, or you are walking alongside someone who has, please know that I wrote this book for *you*. This book is not written from the desk of a psychiatrist, psychologist, pastor, doctor, or grief counselor. No, my education in traumatic grief came from the experience of losing my son, whom we lost to the depths of depression just weeks after his twentieth birthday.

I understand the massive, suffocating agony that threatens to rip your heart from your chest, the confusion that volleys in your soul, and the tormenting questions that haunt you every minute of every day. I'm sorry you have to know this pain. The loss of a loved one to suicide is one of the most painful and traumatic experiences a person can endure. This complicated type of grief is sudden, shocking, and deeply disturbing. In fact, according to the American Psychiatric Association, losing someone to suicide is said to be in the catastrophic range. Please understand that what you have gone through compares in strength to the stress associated with a concentration camp experience.[1]

---

1. Jeffrey Jackson, *A Handbook for Coping with Suicide Grief* (Washington, D.C.: American Association of Suicidology, 2023), 5, https://suicidology.org/wp-content/uploads/2024/11/Handbook_for_Coping_with_Suicide_Grief_06-24.pdf.

This is a book I never hoped to write, and I'm sure this is a book you never hoped to read. But here we are, having been brought together by an unbelievable, tragic pain *not everyone* can understand. Doctors and counselors can "learn" about this type of tragedy in textbooks, but there is an understanding and connection formed through human hearts that have personally endured such agony. *You* are not alone.

This book is a companion willing to walk with you on what is likely the hardest road you will ever travel—a friend who understands the unbelievable agony you've been thrown into and offers advice, encouragement, and hope drawn from my own lived experience. My prayer is that this book can be a guide for you in traversing traumatic grief, surviving a potential crisis in your faith, and overcoming the misinformation, stigma, and judgment often experienced regarding depression and suicide. I pray that reading this book helps you develop a deeper sense of empathy and gain a new perspective, one that brings honor to the memory and legacy of your lost loved one or anyone who has died by suicide.

What follows in these pages is a straightforward, easy-to-read approach in which you'll learn what is common in suicide grief and survival tactics for healing. You will learn to acknowledge and process your grief emotions and how to lay down your guilt. You will learn about the ugly trials I faced during my crisis of faith, which I'm confident can guide you back to God if you ever find yourself in a similar place. I'll share revelations of God that are hard to accept but have great value. I'll help you understand the importance of asking "Why?" You'll learn how to transform your pain, and you'll begin to understand what healing from grief is and isn't. Further, you will see why suicide has substantial stigma, misinformation, and judgments attached to it, which will give you a deeper understanding, empathy, and awareness of this serious health issue.

When my son passed, I was desperate to understand what had happened to this phenomenal young man who had his whole life ahead of him. I buried myself in reading, counseling, and prayer. I devoured books, articles, and resources in hopes of finding comfort, answers, and hope. I wanted to understand depression. I wanted to understand my grief. I wanted to understand the taking of one's own life and where God's Word stood on these issues. In many ways, I found all those things, along with a desire to help you find them as well, precisely because I know the peace they brought me.

As I walked through the unbelievable agony of grief, the gaping hole in my heart was filled with anger, bitterness, and confusion. Not being able to reconcile living as a believer with such tragedy, I fired God from my life. Yet, when I reached the end of myself and found no hope in the world either, I reluctantly turned back to God with bitterness, wrong motives, and anger. And although I thought it was impossible, after much wrestling, questioning, and anguish, I found joy and hope in life again, and I discovered a God I never fully knew.

It is not easy to share particulars of our son's death. But we believe by sharing, we might prevent just one more tragedy. If even one person finds hope, understanding, or healing through our story, then we find deeper healing in turn. It would help us to see that our pain didn't just stop at pain, but it ended in purpose. It would be worth bearing it all if it could encourage anyone else walking through the trenches of hell. With depression on the rise and the fact that worldwide, someone loses their life to suicide every 40 seconds,[2] there has never been a more important time for knowledge and awareness of our mental health and the survival tactics available in these pages.

While this book is written specifically for grievers of suicide, it will also strengthen anyone who struggles with how to help these individuals enduring this traumatic loss. In addition, many sections apply to anyone facing trials, loss, or a crisis of faith, and they also usher in a greater awareness regarding suicide and depression. At the end of each section, you'll find a prayer that you can make your own, if you'd like. To help readers more easily navigate, this book begins with an introduction letter for suicide grievers and one for friends and family. It is then divided into three parts. **Part 1: Our Story: All Too Common** shares not only our son's story, but also my own—the crisis I endured

---

2. "Suicide: One Person Dies Every 40 Seconds," *World Health Organization*, September 9, 2019, https://www.who.int/news/item/09-09-2019-suicide-one-person-dies-every-40-seconds.

in my faith. My prayer is that it gives insight into any doubts you may have. **Part 2: Navigating the Flood of Feelings** shares how to do just that: process all of your feelings while traversing this valley of grief to find hope and healing. Finally, **Part 3: Gaining Clarity and Hope**, deals with suicide stigma, prevention, how to transition from a suicide griever into a suicide survivor, and what to do from here. These three parts are followed by a few important appendices that deal with specific family relationships in grief, a depression self-check list, and a list of recommended resources.

In utilizing the important information in this book for your grief journey, I believe you will find that although our hearts may forever be scarred from our loss, it is possible for us to move forward and live life fully again. I understand if you can't fathom that right now. Just hold on; you can make it through this. There is light at the end of your tunnel. I'll help you find it.

DISCLAIMER

This book is not a comprehensive study, and it is not intended to be used as a diagnostic tool. Rather, this is one family's journey through suicide grief resulting from major depression. Clinical assessment is needed to determine any mental health issues. This book is intended to support, comfort, and inform grieving families and provide awareness, advocacy, and empathy surrounding the issues of depression and the taking of one's own life. Please make sure to see a healthcare provider immediately if there is any suspicion that you or someone you know may be depressed or suicidal. My first recommendation would be to call the Christians in Crisis hotline at 1-844-472-9687. Another option is the 9-8-8 suicide and mental health hotline, which is designed to be a quick and memorable number to connect those who are hurting with help. A counseling tool like GriefShare is recommended if you are experiencing grief from the loss of a loved one.

Dear Fellow
Griever of Suicide
(You'll want to read this.)

We likely don't understand the depth of pain our loved ones were in, just as they could never have known the depth of pain losing them would cause.
—Victoria Myers

Dear Fellow Griever of Suicide,

We share a monstrous pain, a soul-crushing tragedy, and an unbelievable loss. I'm sorry you have to know this pain. Suicide assuredly has to be one of the most horrific ways to lose a loved one. You are not alone. I know after my loss, I desperately needed answers for my survival, for my very sanity. I needed to hear from others who had lived through this type of tragedy. To be honest, I was shocked anyone could. I truly felt I would die from my grief. I desperately needed hope. Right now, I want you to know you *can* survive, and *you will*.

On top of the usual grief associated with a conventional loss, we have an added load of trauma and emotional turmoil that is unique to death by suicide.[1] One common name for us is "suicide survivors"

---

1. Jackson, *A Handbook for Coping with Suicide Grief*, 1.

because our experience comprises trauma and a myriad of emotions, including confusion, bias, judgment, stigma, unfinished business, guilt, blame, exclusion, abandonment, and a disconnect that doesn't generally come with a conventional loss. "Suicide is particularly traumatizing because we do not know how to resolve our hurt and outrage. If it had been a murder, we could grieve for the victim and vent our rage at the murderer. Yet, as suicide grievers, we grieve the loved one we lost to suicide and rage against him simultaneously."[2] Suicide grief is just different. Suicide grief is complicated.

A year before we lost our son, we lost my husband's dad, who passed away suddenly from a brain bleed. But as devastating as that loss was, the intensity of trauma and pain we experienced in losing our son to suicide hit a depth of grief and trauma we didn't know existed until it happened to us. My husband himself pointed this out.

We were in shock for at least the first month or two after losing our son. You may be also. It's unbelievable and surreal. It's like you're in an alternate reality, and you can't wait to wake up to your normal life again. You may zone out and stare off into space. You may, like me, keep saying things like, "I just can't believe this," over and over again. Shock is a survival tactic that helps numb us to the severe emotional pain for a time, just so we can function. These feelings of shock can sometimes be strong enough to trigger PTSD (post-traumatic stress disorder). In fact, according to author Albert Y. Hsu, the American Psychiatric Association ranks the stress of losing a loved one to suicide as "catastrophic"—equivalent to that of a concentration camp experience.[3] I hope this helps you see the level of stress that you're enduring. Right now, it's important to take it just one day at a time, perhaps one hour at a time.

You may want someone to drive you places the first few weeks— honestly, it can be dangerous to drive. In early grief, your mind feels detached, and you're not fully present. I remember the first time I got behind the wheel alone after losing our son. I was driving home, and

---

2. Albert Y. Hsu, *Grieving a Suicide: A Loved One's Search for Comfort, Answers, and Hope* (Illinois: InterVarsity Press, 2017), 35.
3. Ibid., 10.

halfway there, I started to have a panic attack. I had to pull over to the side of the road because I thought I was going to pass out from hyperventilating. My husband had to come and get me. If I hadn't been alone, I think it wouldn't have happened at all.

Don't allow others to put you in situations you can't handle at this time. If there was something I knew I couldn't handle, I wouldn't do it. The second or third week, we tried to go back to church. We only made it to the parking lot, turned around, and went back home because I couldn't go in. Some family members may be ready to join in on certain activities, while others may not. Let each person grieve in their own way.

The suicide of your loved one is not something you'll *just* get over. Knowing how to deal with traumatic grief *does not* come naturally. In nearly every area of life, we are all wiser when we look to those who have been there before us. The death of a loved one to suicide is no different. Some are trained in how to aid you, and others can guide you because they have experienced it firsthand. Allow us both to help you navigate this grief.

IT WASN'T SUICIDE!

Losing someone to suicide is so surreal. It's almost impossible to wrap your head around the idea that your loved one could take their own life. I understand—this realization is so hard to grasp and so painful to even consider. After all, the natural instinct of every human is to cling to life and fight for survival. When this natural drive is overpowered, it not only points to the depth of the struggle going on inside, but it also helps us begin to understand why it feels so impossible for us to believe.

For at least the first year or more, we went back and forth from accepting it to not believing it at all. My husband even called up the sheriff multiple times, wanting him to reexamine the evidence. At first, we all believed it must have been an accident. We played out different scenarios over and over in our minds. We then morphed into believing that someone might have murdered him, again playing out scenarios about who it might have been and how they might have gotten away with it. But we finally had to admit he wasn't the type of person to have enemies.

Then, there were his future plans. If he'd been planning for his future, surely he wouldn't have ended his life. The very night of his death, he had made plans with a group of friends for the following week. And the day before, he had ordered some motorcycle parts to finish a repair he was doing on his dirt bike. But we found out it's actually common for suicide victims to have been making plans for the future. According to professor of psychology Thomas Joiner, there is a constant struggle "with competing forces tugging at the suicidal individual from the sides of both life and death."[4] They don't want to die, yet they often see no other way out of their daunting mental anguish.

It took a very long time for many in our family to believe it was anything other than an accident, and honestly, some may very well *still* believe this to be true. But as I started to read and research, I found that family and friends of a suicide victim usually deny it was death by suicide. You don't want to believe it, no matter how much evidence there is. My husband, especially, wanted to believe it was an accident instead of suicide, but as I shared more and more information and research with him, he started to see the unmistakable signs of our son's major depression and, sadly, the unmistakable signs of death by suicide. You are not alone if you long so badly for another possibility to be true.

SHOCK WAVES

After the loss of my son, I would often be fine one minute and then jarred into an awareness of the way he died the next. I would shudder and suck in air, almost as if it were hitting me again for the first time. This experience continued well into the second year. It's as if the utter trauma of it all is too much to take at once, so our bodies only focus on the reality of it for so long. For that reason, the jarring awareness delivers its overwhelming torment in small doses. Bit by bit. Here,

---

4. Thomas Joiner, *Myths about Suicide* (Massachusetts: Harvard University Press, 2010), 64.

then there. This wasn't the same as the grief waves of sadness that would hit, but an entirely different experience that came only because of *how* he died; so, instead of calling them grief waves, I call them shock waves. I didn't understand this strange phenomenon, and I had never heard a word that explained what it was exactly. Just know that if you are experiencing this too, you are not alone.

PROCESSING YOUR THOUGHTS AND EMOTIONS

Right now, your brain is likely stuck on recycling all those thoughts of your loved one and how they passed. You keep replaying the events over and over. I'm sorry. This is normal. It will get better. It may take months and months, but it will get better. I experienced and later read that as suicide grievers, even if we didn't personally witness the scene, we often play out what we imagine the scene to have been like.[5] I too experienced this. This is a normal part of traumatic grief. We so badly want to change the outcome of what happened. I feel like our brains are stuck on replay because we believe that if we think about it long enough, we can reason it away somehow or find a solution. I've heard it said that it's as if our brain has knowledge of the loss, but our heart isn't ready to accept it. This unbalanced understanding will start to level out, but it will take time.

Sometimes, my grief felt so scary and incomprehensible that I was afraid to ever let it go at full throttle. How would I react? Would I...go crazy? What would it look like? How would others respond? Would I even scare myself?

Further, you'll deal with anger. Find a safe outlet to release it—it may be good for you. I so badly wanted to get a baseball bat and demolish a car. (Not the best option.) And since there wasn't a car I could get away with smashing, I had to find another outlet. One day, on a walk in the field by our house, I picked up a large limb and beat a tree trunk raw. I did feel a little better afterward.

One night, my husband needed to release some anger. He went to

---

5. Beverly Cobain and Jean Larch, *Dying to Be Free: A Healing Guide for Families After a Suicide* (Minnesota: Hazelden, 2006), 55.

the basketball goal near our driveway and literally pulled it out of the ground and chucked it across the yard. Anger, in traumatic grief, is normal.

You may also experience strange thoughts that aren't a part of your normal character. For example, when I would go out, I looked at people and wondered, *Why are all these people still alive, but my son isn't? Why couldn't it have been them who got sick?*

Never in all my life before this had I imagined such soul-crushing pain existed. During the grief, I often thought, *It's not fair that some have pain this deep and others never experience it.* The worst thought I had was, *Everyone should have to experience this just once.* You may have thoughts like this or thoughts you consider to be even worse. It's tempting to think that having these thoughts is horrible, that those are not things that should come to a Christian's mind, but it's normal in grief. It's okay. You have most likely just gone through one of the hardest trials of your life—be forgiving of yourself. Your mind is blinded with anguish, anger, bitterness, and grief. It's normal to feel bitter. This, too, you will lay down bit by bit.

Don't Give Up: Instead Get Help

You may become exhausted in every way possible, completely spent—physically, emotionally, mentally, spiritually, and relationally—all of them, all at once. This, too, will ease up, come and go, and perhaps come again, but it will eventually pass. Take it easy on yourself in the meantime.

Grief is like traveling through a minefield, never knowing when you'll take an explosive step. But these steps aren't wrong, because each step needs to be taken. You can make it through this battlefield of grief. But along the way, you'll encounter many hidden minefields—sights, sounds, smells, memories, and even finding your loved one's old sock can cause you to break down.

I heard so many people say, "You need to be strong right now," but I think the best thing you can do right now is to be open to grief. It's okay to be sad. God gave us a built-in pressure release valve called tears. It's okay to cry. Grief is *natural.* Grief is *okay.* Grief is *needed.*

Trying to muster strength that isn't there is like tying yourself in knots, fighting against what your body naturally needs.

Suicide grief is murky, uncharted territory. It's such a fearful experience. I wanted to lock the rest of my family in a bubble, never to expose them to the risks of life again. You might be scared to live, too. You wonder how you will ever get past this frozen state. But slowly, if only drop by drop, the iceberg of fear will melt. Hold on. Day by day, the fear will recede.

My guess is that right now, you want to crawl into bed. Or maybe you're already there, and you may hope you'll never crawl out again. I understand. I've been there. I hoped to lie there and die after the loss of my son. You can see two paths. And you so badly want to take the one that seems less exhausting and less painful. If you're experiencing these types of feelings, please share them with someone and avoid being alone. The only thing that made me get out of my bed of grief was knowing my son wouldn't want that end for me. And I had other loved ones I needed to go on for. I'm sure your family and friends feel the same about you. Please, don't give up. You can make it through this day. Then the next and the next and the next. It's a slow process, and it hurts like hell, but the intensity of these feelings will slowly dissipate.

You don't have to do it alone. It is important to get outside help. If money is an issue, we found a healthy and amazingly helpful free program called GriefShare. It is administered through a video seminar, group discussion (you don't have to speak if you don't want to), and a personal workbook. While it's offered to the public in over 8,500 churches nationwide, you do not have to be a Christian to go through the program. This program is an asset to *anyone* who is grieving. Needing outside help is okay. In fact, in traumatic grief, I believe it is essential. Our whole family attended the GriefShare program, and we all benefited from it. I can't recommend it enough. Find a group near you at www.griefshare.org. I would also suggest reading other books on suicide grief, too, or joining a suicide grief support group in person or online.

Initially, I had the urge to emotionally retreat and hide what happened to my son. I could have lived, never saying a word to anyone, whether they were in my inner circle or the outer world. That urge to hide it all was so tempting. But I never had the chance. To heal, my husband *needed* to talk about it with everyone we knew. (Some find healing in talking about it.) Part of his compulsion to tell the story might have been a subconscious way to protect me from having to tell it. Telling it more than the two times I initially had to tell it might have caused a mental and emotional breakdown. Only later, through my reading and counseling, did I learn it's best not to try to conceal the cause of this type of loss for many reasons. The most prominent is that even if you succeed at never saying a word, the secret will eventually destroy you, or it will surface unexpectedly. We also learned that many suicide grievers don't tell children, but when the child finds out the truth later, they will have to grieve twice over the same loss. This is often more damaging in the long run.[6]

I quite seriously considered moving away. It seemed it would make things easier somehow. Yet, it wasn't a realistic option because of my husband's work. (Counseling let us know it's important not to make major life decisions in the first year after loss.) Now I can see staying was probably best for our healing. Running away might have been easier at first, but it likely would have left unhealed places in our hearts. We can't heal what we don't acknowledge.

Leaving your church might be a temptation, as well. Statistically, at least 80 percent of people who lose loved ones to suicide will either quit church altogether or switch to a new church within two years of the loss.[7] We stuck it out and are glad we did because it has been a comfort to stay in an environment where almost everyone knew and loved our son. I would encourage you to stay the course.

I know many struggle to tell the truth of their loved one's passing,

---

6. Hsu, *Grieving a Suicide*, 53–54.

7. David B. Biebel and Suzanne L. Foster, *Finding Your Way After the Suicide of Someone You Love* (Grand Rapids: Zondervan, 2005), 169.

for fear of what others may think or how they may react. I was not above that trepidation. Some fear this so badly they may switch doctors or hairstylists; they may change normal life patterns so they won't have to tell this person or that. But one thing I can tell you is there is a level of peace that comes in knowing you've told the truth of your loved one's passing. At first, in grief, it may not seem like it, but as time passes, you can breathe deeper knowing the truth has been told and your future isn't marked with keeping such a huge lie alive. More importantly, processing your grief honestly helps you heal. And, as you'll see in subsequent chapters, speaking up and telling the truth helps to demolish the stigma surrounding mental health. Even more, we need to get out of this mindset that telling the truth of our loved one's suicide somehow diminishes them; instead, the truth of our loved one's death helps to acknowledge the depth of their pain and honor their struggle. Their story deserves to be told.

SUICIDE AND FREE WILL: UNDERSTANDING THE PAIN

One of the most painful aspects of losing a loved one to suicide is wrestling with the question of whether it was their choice. Did they really choose this? Could they have chosen differently? These are haunting thoughts that can lead to anger, confusion, and bitterness. If there is one thing I hope to convey, it is this: suicide is rarely a decision made in the way we typically understand choice.

In *Night Falls Fast: Understanding Suicide*, Kay Redfield Jamison highlights the overwhelming prevalence of mental illness among those who die by suicide, a fact echoed in numerous studies. Research indicates that 90 to 95 percent of individuals who die by suicide likely had an underlying mental health condition at the time of their death.[8] Among these, roughly 60 percent suffered from major depression[9], while many

8. Kay Redfield Jamison, *Night Falls Fast* (New York: Alfred A. Knopf, 1999), 100.
9. HealthyPlace, "Facts About Suicide," accessed March 5, 2025, https://www.healthy place.com/bipolar-disorder/articles/facts-about-sucide.

others battled bipolar disorder or other severe mental health struggles.[10]

While most suicides appear to be driven by mental health issues, I acknowledge that there may be rare instances when someone takes their life for reasons that don't fit this pattern. However, research and personal testimonies indicate that, for many, suicide is not about a rational, calculated decision. Instead, their suffering or illness distorts their perception so severely that they see no other way out. Recognizing this complexity allows us to approach suicide loss with more compassion, understanding, and grace, both toward our loved ones and toward ourselves.

Let's consider those who engage in self-harm, such as cutting. Most would agree this is not a healthy or logical behavior but rather an attempt to cope with emotional distress, trauma, or overwhelming pain. Often, the intent is not to cause harm but to find relief. Similarly, many who die by suicide may not be choosing death in the way we typically think of choices; rather, they are seeking an end to suffering through the only means their hurting, overwhelmed minds can conceive. The American Association of Suicidology states, "Based on the accounts of those who have attempted suicide and lived to tell about it, we know that the primary goal of a suicide is not to end their life, but to end the pain."[11]

Why does this distinction of choice matter? Because understanding the depth of a loved one's suffering can bring a sense of peace. It can help ease feelings of anger or guilt, replacing them with greater empathy and healing. And it matters for those still struggling with suicidal thoughts. If we speak about suicide solely as a personal choice, it can place an even heavier burden on those who are battling these thoughts, making them feel misunderstood, ashamed, or hopeless.[12]

---

10. Healthline, "Are Suicide Rates Higher for People with Bipolar Disorder?" accessed March 5, 2025, https://www.healthline.com/health/suicide-and-bipolar.

11. Jackson, *A Handbook for Survivors of Suicide,* 10.

12. John Ackerman, "Don't Say It's Selfish: Suicide Is Not a Choice," Nationwide Children's Hospital, February 15, 2024, https://www.nationwidechildrens.org/family-resources-education/700childrens/2019/11/suicide-is-not-a-choice.

Instead, when we acknowledge the complexity of suicide, we create space for compassion, support, and more effective intervention.

I don't pretend to have all the answers, and I can't tell you what to believe about your loved one's experience. I knew my son's heart, and the last thing he would ever want to do is hurt anyone. I believe what happened to him wasn't a clear-headed decision, but a heartbreaking moment of desperation that grew out of a long season of pain and hopelessness. My purpose in sharing this is not to impose my perspective on you but to offer insight that may help you process your loss. If you are struggling with these questions, I encourage you to extend yourself the same grace you would offer someone else, because suicide grief is complex, and there are some questions we may never have definitive answers to.

TROUBLED MINDS: WHY DID THEY DO IT?

Why? Those of us who have lost a loved one to death by suicide want that answer more than ever in life. It just doesn't make sense, but really, it shouldn't. Suicide isn't a sensible thing. Still, grievers of suicide think that if we just understand the *why*, we'd feel more settled.[13]

You often hear people's self-important theories[14]: "It was because he lost his job," "It was because her boyfriend broke up with her," "It was because of this or that." But there is no *one* reason. Suicide is usually not a sudden decision, but rather the result of feelings of hopelessness that have been building for a long time. Someone who is mentally and emotionally *well* is not going to want to take their own life because of *one* bad incident. "The fact that medication can often prevent suicide should tell us something."[15] No, there is way more going on inside a suicidal mind than just a bad life event.

We search for answers from our deceased loved ones themselves—any clues among their things, a letter they wrote, or something they said or did that may help us understand the *why*. I once came across a

13. Hsu, *Grieving a Suicide*, 86.
14. Jackson, *A Handbook for Coping with Suicide Grief*, 4.
15. Ronald Rolheiser, *Bruised and Wounded: Struggling to Understand Suicide* (Massachusetts: Paraclete Press, 2018), 19.

statement I can't fully source, but that stayed with me: Even if there is a suicide letter, the troubled mind that died from suicide is the same troubled mind that wrote the letter.[16] Letters can be more misleading than informative because they may lead you to assume the victim knew what they were doing. Since mental illness is so prevalent in suicide victims, even with a letter, the victim may not have understood what was happening to them.[17] I imagine the best thing to do with any notes or journals left behind would be to talk about them with a reputable, professional counselor who has testimonies from people they've helped through a similar trauma. I was glad there was no such letter in our case. It wouldn't have made any sense, no matter what it said, because nothing would make the loss of my son's life make sense. A letter might have only compounded the pain.

Our loved ones' thoughts were misinformed. Their problems seemed impossible to overcome. And although *we* could easily see love, hope, and a future for them, they couldn't see any of that for themselves. Can you imagine having absolutely no hope in anything or anyone? Period. What a very dark and scary place! Essentially, unimaginable and daunting mental anguish, coupled with absolutely no hope for anything, is likely the answer to the *why*. And although we might not fully understand our loved one's suicide, recognizing the very real possibility that they were *ill* can help us find healing for ourselves.

When You Blame Yourself

One thing I learned is that whether you are a parent, sibling, best friend, significant other, cousin, grandparent, or any loved one, you will blame yourself.[18] "If only I had called." "If only I had stayed later." "If I hadn't left him alone." Realize that no matter when it happened, there would likely be a new *if only*. There are so many reasons we can find to blame ourselves, especially if the death occurred after a parent's punishment or a couple's fight, or a similar conflict. But these accusa-

---

16. Original source no longer known; included here in recognition that the idea is not uniquely mine.
17. Jackson, *SOS A Handbook for Coping with Suicide Grief*, 11.
18. Ibid., 15.

tions are pointless and harmful.[19] You didn't realize until it was too late that your loved one had reached a point of no return. You tell yourself you didn't love them well enough.

But here's the truth:

It's
not
your
fault!

Mental illness or distorted thinking, not your actions or lack thereof, likely was the cause of their death.

In her book, *Night Falls Fast,* Dr. Kay Redfield Jamison, a psychiatrist who has struggled with bipolar depression, shares her perception of personal relationships during her bipolar depression:

> No amount of love from or for other people—and there was a lot—could help. No advantage of a caring family and fabulous job was enough to overcome the pain and hopelessness I felt; no passionate or romantic love, however strong, could make a difference. Nothing alive and warm could make its way in through my carapace. . . . In fact, I'd venture to say [those suffering from suicidal thoughts] are too entrenched in psychological pain to even think of anyone else at the time.[20]

Similarly, Drew, a young Christian man, had good, attentive parents and an active life, yet that didn't stop him from jumping off a bridge one night as he was sucked under by suicidal despair. Drew's father was a counselor to teens and college students, and although he and Drew's mother knew he suffered from depression, his suicidal nosedive went unnoticed due to his active, overachiever lifestyle. Thankfully, Drew survived his jump from the bridge and had these important words to share:

---

19. Adina Wrobleski, *Suicide Survivors: A Guide for Those Left Behind* (Minneapolis: Suicide Awareness Voices of Education, 1991), 59.
20. Jamison, *Night Falls Fast*, 291.

I knew my family loved me, and I loved them, but the suicide feelings overtook my love for my family and their love for me. The suicide feelings were just stronger than the love.[21]

Hearing these personal accounts helped me better understand the state of mind my son likely was in. Even though we had shared good times as recently as that last week, he might have been oblivious to our love. Only God truly knows the state of mind and the intents of the heart of each individual who takes their own life. *No one* is at fault when suicide comes by way of mental illness any more than someone is at fault for Alzheimer's disease or type 1 diabetes.

Who are we to judge their motives, their hearts, or their minds?

When guilt arises, redirect your thoughts. Remember times when your love and actions made a positive impact on their life. This will help reinforce the truth that it was not your one act or omission that was the cause of their death.[22] In addition, Albert Hsu, an author and suicide loss survivor suggests it may help to ask for your loved one's forgiveness—perhaps at their gravesite—or write them a letter expressing what's on your heart. These things can help release guilt and foster healing.[23] Similarly, I wrote a letter to my son, pouring out all the things I wished I had told him: how much he meant to us, how deeply we loved him, and how sorry I was that I didn't fully understand what he was going through. This did bring me a measure of closure. It gave me an outlet to express all those unspoken words, but it also gave me a way to apologize and let him know how important he was to us.

You may still have regrets for how you treated your loved one at times or the words you once said. A fellow griever, Louise, shared this profound insight: "Through prayer, I have come to realize that I cannot judge what I did back then with the information I have now. I gave myself permission to be a 'normal parent' and make mistakes with my son, as all parents do."[24] No one can judge what they did in a rela-

21. David Cox and Candy Arrington, *Aftershock: Help, Hope, and Healing in the Wake of Suicide* (B&H Books, 2003), 42.
22. Wrobleski, *Suicide Survivors*, 83.
23. Hsu, *Grieving a Suicide*, 109.
24. Biebel and Foster, *Finding Your Way*, 42.

tionship before someone's passing with the information they now have. You have to give yourself permission to be a normal brother or sister, a normal aunt or uncle, or even a normal friend. We are all imperfect, but our love is true.

Maria, my GriefShare leader, was quick to remind us that "those last words (or actions), even if they weren't perfect, did not have the power to destroy the whole life and relationship you had with your loved one." I know this will bring comfort to you, too. The last minutes, days, or even months of a loved one's life should not take precedence over the years of love you shared before.

David Biebel, doctor of ministry, and Suzanne Foster, licensed therapist, shared some of the most healing words:

> Healing involves making peace with the past and accepting that you did the best you could with the knowledge you had at the time. It means realizing how little control you had over events, circumstances, and the actions of others and accepting that there may not have been anything you could have done to affect the outcome. Sometimes, all the love in the world can't fill the emptiness another person has inside nor change their feelings of confusion and despair.[25]

Please hear me, friend; your loved one's death is not your fault.

WHAT COULD POSSIBLY BE NEXT?

You're still in an intense time of struggle, shock, and fear. Any suggestion that you might accept what has happened and move forward with your life might horrify you. How can you keep living when the one you love so much is gone? It's okay to feel that way. It's okay if recovering feels impossible or even wrong to think about right now. That doesn't mean you never will recover—but know that it's also okay if, at some point, that begins to change. The journey of grief can be a very long road that is unpredictable and different for everyone.

---

25. Ibid., 148.

Like I did, you may have so much anger, fear, and guilt that they are multiplying the pain of the loss itself. When you are ready, hand it over to God. The pain of the loss itself is enough. And you honor your loved one more by choosing to live to the fullest rather than keeping the wound from healing. You can survive, and you will. And although it may be hard to feel God, by His promise, He is there with you. (Take heart, while some of the most daunting questions have been touched on in this initial section, we will look at many of these subjects in greater depth throughout this book.)

Dear God,

I'm in a place I cannot even fathom. What happened? How can this be true? I can't believe my loved one is gone. I wake up each day having to relive this horrible reality. Fear has gripped me and has a stranglehold on me. God, You're going to have to help me know I can live again, because right now it seems completely impossible. This feels beyond repair. My heart weighs five thousand pounds and threatens to rip itself from my chest. Lord, help me to be open to the truth of Your love because I don't feel it right now. Lord, I believe; help my unbelief. Give me understanding to remain still and trust You. Give me the faith to see the possibility that my loved one is safe in Your arms with no more pain.

In Jesus's name, amen.

Dear Family and Friends, In the Fight

The deeper the pain, the fewer the words.
—Rick Warren

Dear Family and Friends, in the Fight,

If you are reading this, it must be that a family member or friend has lost a loved one to suicide, and you wish to not only understand their pain but also to walk with them through it. Thank you for your love and courage to enter the valley with them.

Why This Is a Hard Place to Tread

In dealing with others' loss, perhaps you initially wanted to avoid your family or friends altogether for fear you wouldn't know what to do or say, or you're worried you might unintentionally hurt them more. I understand this. Before my loss, I must admit I tried my best to avoid people in such deep pain and loss. You want to help, but then you are afraid you'll hurt them more instead by saying or doing the wrong thing. Let me share some things with you that I learned through this deep pain, which may encourage you.

The Deeper the Pain, the Fewer the Words

One of the best things I heard regarding helping our loved ones who have lost someone came from Rick Warren in an interview on TBN after sharing about the loss of his son to suicide. He said one of the most important things to let friends and family know is this: "The deeper the pain, the fewer the words!" I believe this is so true. The deeper the perception of loss or trauma, the fewer the words that need to be said and the fewer the words that want to be heard. For example, it may not be true in every case, but it is most likely that the loss of a child is a deeper pain than the loss of grandparents; therefore, the harder the grief, the deeper the likelihood of bitterness, confusion, and pain. Rick Warren went on to say, "You show up and shut up." Just being there is what he calls "the ministry of presence."[1]

David Biebel shares some great wisdom as well, which carries the same sentiment. In the book he wrote after losing his young son, he shared, "I think it is safe to say that the most effective comforting comes through things done for, rather than things said to, a bereaved person, especially early in the grieving process."[2] This should bring some comfort in knowing you don't have to know what to say or even feel obligated to say anything.

Just
show
up.

What *Not* to Do:

- Do not try to offer a reason for the suicide.
- Do not ask for details of the suicide.
- Do not say, "I know so-and-so had this happen in their

---

1. YouTube, "Rick Warren Testimony: My Son Matthew's Suicide & How Ministry Flows from Deep Pain," interview by Matt and Laurie Crouch, *Praise on TBN,* May 4, 2021, video, 11:22, https://www.youtube.com/watch?v=HCUbog65dP4.

2. David B. Biebel, *Jonathon: You Left Too Soon* (Florida: Healthy Life Press, 2012), 140.

family, but it was worse because..." Each loss is unique, and
you have no way to gauge the depth of someone's loss.

- Do not make harmful statements such as "It was their
choice" or "It was selfish of them."
- Do not say, "I know how you feel." Even if you've
experienced suicide loss yourself, you cannot fully
understand another's grief or the unique bond they shared
with their loved one—only God can know that.

How to Mourn with Those Who Mourn

Aside from the story of Job, the Bible doesn't seem to give friends or
family much advice on how to help in times of mourning, but it does
clearly show friends and family went and mourned with their loved
ones who had lost someone. It does tell us to "mourn with those who
mourn" (Romans 12:15 NIV).

So, what does it look like to mourn with those who mourn? I'll
share a few examples that happened with the loss of our son. One
included how a deacon in our church reacted when he prayed for me
shortly after our son's passing. He mourned with me. It wasn't just a
few silent tears that rolled off his cheeks. It was sobbing that reverber-
ated his body. It was praying aloud with his voice quivering and his
body shaking. I could tell that he was feeling our pain. He was truly
mourning with us. Another touching expression of grief came from a
soul sister of mine, who I heard collapsed to her knees when she
learned the news of Haden's passing. These touched me deeply. This
let me know not only their love for my son but also the heartbreak
they shared with us.

So often, people come to a grieving family and think, *I have to be
strong for them.* No, you don't. I believe one of the single best things you
can do is express your emotions. Mourn with them. And allow them to
express their emotions. This lets them know you loved the one they
lost, and you love them. I believe God placed a healing element within
this mutual mourning—one that can only be released as the mourning
is shared.

One dear friend stepped in and helped our family by finding the closest grief support group, which turned out to be our GriefShare group. She called, gathered all the information we needed, and passed it along to me. Although I knew we needed help, I was too exhausted and likely mentally and emotionally unable to get it together enough to find this on my own.

Family friends gifted us a tree in remembrance of our son. They asked what type of tree we wanted, and I chose a maple blaze because my son loved autumn, mostly because it was hunting season. This is a special memorial for my son, which will live in my yard for years to come. I had planned to get a tree myself at some point, but it became even more special when family friends thought to get it for us. Not only did they purchase it, but they delivered it and helped us plant it. We then stood around it holding hands, and they prayed for us.

A deeply moving gesture of mourning that honored my son came from a respected elder, who shared that he had placed a photo of our son on his personal "wall of heroes" in his home. Knowing they have a picture in their home to mark remembrance and love for our son was so special and showed they *truly* knew my Haden's heart.

There was another friend who was always checking up on me via text, or she was sending something in the mail, including pictures she had found of Haden. She gave me books she thought would help with healing. She would come and take our younger son to do fun activities with her boy, or pick our son up so he wouldn't miss events. This helped because, while I wasn't ready to take him, he could still choose to go if he wanted.

Mourning with us included family and friends who came and stayed with us. It was those who helped us add special touches to Haden's celebration of life. Those who pulled late nights to get slideshows done and the music just right. It was those who organized meals so we didn't have to worry about anything. It was those who weren't afraid to burst out crying because they knew we understood they, too, were hurting and mourning the loss of our son. It was those who weren't afraid to mention our son's name to tell a story about him that made us smile. Those who swept my floor and even cleaned out my fridge to make room for more food. It was those who simply came. Sat. Cried.

Hugged. These, my friend, are examples of mourning with those who mourn. While some of these gestures may seem simple, when your world has been torn apart, they mean everything. And let me reassure you: *you* can offer this kind of comfort, too.

I know perhaps you are scared to go, scared you'll say the wrong thing, do the wrong thing. And perhaps you will, but I promise they will know you are trying to love them and that you care. They will know that despite the awkwardness or fear, you came to love them. They will know their lost loved one held a special place in your heart, as well. Further, remember that God has called us each to mourn with those who mourn. We must remember that if He has called us to it, He will equip us for it.

How to Best Comfort Those Who Have Lost a Child

One of the most touching, healing, and helpful things I experienced was only a few words my nephew spoke to me at the viewing. It touched my heart as he told me what wonderful parents we had been to Haden, that we had raised Haden right, that we had done right by him, and that he was such a good young man. He went on to say he looked up to Haden even though he was the older cousin. It was as if he, if even just a little, added a stitch to the gaping hole in my heart with those words. Family and friends, if your loved one has lost a child, one of the single best things you can do for them is reassure them that they were good parents and that they did well in loving their children, because as a parent grieves their lost child, the guilt and worry that this *wasn't true* is so overwhelming it threatens to engulf them.

The Best Gifts You Can Give

Without a doubt, pictures are such a beautiful gift, especially if they're pictures of the lost loved one the family has never seen before. We had many people send pictures to us digitally. I think something even more special would be if you framed and gave them the pictures in printed form, since nowadays, we keep so few printed pictures.

While a picture is worth a thousand words, sometimes words are the most lasting gift. Sharing stories of the lost loved one, especially those the family may have never heard, means more than you know. They offer a glimpse into parts of their life lived outside the family's view, moments that reveal just how deeply they touched others. And while sharing these memories aloud is a beautiful gift, writing them down can be even more powerful. A letter filled with these stories becomes something they can return to again and again, a reminder that their loved one's life was wide, beautiful, and meaningful.

Special Gestures You Can Share

Here are some ways to support a grieving friend or family member—some we experienced ourselves and found incredibly helpful, and others I later learned would have made a real difference.

If your friend apologizes for crying or breaking down at unexpected moments, reassure them that it's okay. Simple words such as, "It's important to cry," can give them freedom for their grief to flow freely without shame.

Don't ask what you can do, just do what you see needs to be done. In the shock of early grief, even basic tasks can feel impossible. Feeding pets, mowing the lawn, taking out the trash, or checking the mail may not seem like much, but stepping in with these small acts can carry a weight off the grieving person's shoulders.

In the days and weeks following the funeral, when others have returned to their normal lives, be intentional about visiting. The loneliness after the funeral often hits hardest then, and having someone stop by to be with you can mean more than words.

Food is always appreciated, but the way it is delivered can make a difference. Meals sent in disposable containers spare the family from having to track down and return dishes later. If food is being coordinated through a church or group, it's helpful to designate one person to gather and return any containers that are to be returned to the owner.

Another gift of kindness is helping with thank-you notes. I learned this from Elizabeth B. Brown in Surviving the Loss of a Child. She suggests creating one thank-you letter that can be copied and sent to friends and family. Handwriting individual notes when you are already emotionally exhausted can feel like an impossible task, and the worry about whether your words made sense only adds to the weight. Providing help with this process—or encouraging your friend to use a single heartfelt letter—can lift a huge burden.

It's also important to remember that grief cannot be rushed. Each loss is unique, and so is each person's way of grieving. For many, the most intense pain comes during the first year, but the second year can sometimes be even harder. Well-meaning friends often try to hurry others along, attempting to minimize or "fix" grief, but healing doesn't work that way. Grief is not something to avoid; it is a necessary part of the restoration process. Scripture calls us to "mourn with those who mourn," and it offers no timeline for when that should end. Although, while it is important to be patient, it is also wise to remain watchful. If a grieving friend or family member seems downright hopeless, isolated, or unable to engage with life, gently encourage them to seek help—whether through a pastor, counselor, or a support group such as Grief-Share.org.

Sometimes, grieving people also have concern about how other family members are handling their loss. If your friend is upset about how someone else is grieving, remind them that everyone's process looks different and that it's important to give space for those differences. In the same way, don't be afraid to talk about the person who has died. Sharing stories or memories often brings comfort, even when it brings tears. A gentle way to approach this is by asking, "I have a story about [name]. Would you like to hear it now, or save it for later?"

In all of these gestures, remember that grief is deeply personal. What comforts one person may overwhelm another. Some may long to look at photos and share stories, while others may not be ready for that at all. Both responses are okay. Above all, your care and presence mean far more than getting everything "right."

For us, every text, call, card, bouquet, meal, thought, and prayer was like a lifeline. When you are too weak to do anything physically, mentally, relationally, and spiritually, you need others standing in prayer for you. Sometimes, you even need others there just to make logical decisions for you. We are forever grateful for the love family and friends shared with us and the honor they paid to our son, Haden.

I was so thankful for those who stood beside us and were there lifting us up as we stumbled along, injured and broken. It reminds me of a wounded soldier on the battlefield, unable to reach safety. Wounded. Vulnerable. Disoriented. Many family members and friends came, not knowing what they would experience on this battlefield of grief. Perhaps they were worried they wouldn't know what to say or do. But we are so grateful they came anyway, choosing to stand beside us come what may. Because, in all honesty, we were scared, too. We didn't know what to say, either. We were confused. We didn't know what would cause the next tsunami wave of grief to come gushing from our bodies. But we treasure the fact that they loved us enough to find out with us. We could never repay those who mourned with us for their love, but we will never stop trying.

And I imagine this is how your grieving friend or family member will feel about you: deeply grateful that you chose to stand beside them, even when you didn't know what to say or do. Sweet family member or friend, *you* can do this. There has likely never been a time when they need you more than *now*. It may be one of the hardest things you have ever done, but I can promise it will be one of the most meaningful things you have ever done. God will equip you as you seek Him.

Dear God,

Lord, I need Your help, now. My loved one has lost someone so dear, and I don't know what to do. I can't imagine their pain, so how can I hope to comfort them? I don't want to hurt them even more. I am grieving, too, Lord, but I understand their pain runs deeper than mine. Please heal my heart as I stand beside them in this devastating loss. God, I know You will grant me what I need because You have called me to step out and mourn with those who mourn. Help me, Lord, to love them and comfort them as You do. Remind me that I don't need to have all the answers; help me to be slow to speak and quick to listen. Help me to allow them to weep freely and give me the courage to weep with them. Lord, I pray they will turn to You for comfort, strength, healing, and hope.

In Jesus's mighty name I pray, amen.

PART ONE

WHEN THE UNTHINKABLE BECOMES YOUR REALITY

CHAPTER 1

OUR STORY

A LOSS SHARED BY TOO MANY

Talk about them. Be proud of them.
Losing a courageous battle doesn't make you weak.
—Jennifer Betts[1]

"If you knew Haden, you knew you were gonna talk about God. I promise you that. He would go out of his way to make you feel loved." Our family friend Bobby stood at the front of the church, tall and slim with a buzz cut, one hand in his pocket, the other clutching a mic as he fought to maintain his composure. His Southern drawl was saturated in empathy. "I can't tell you how many times Haden prayed for me. Every time he prayed for me, he said, 'I love you, Bob.'"

As much as my heart shook inside me like a traumatized child, I knew Bobby hurt, too. He had been like a second father to Haden. His son, Nick, was Haden's lifelong best friend. Behind Bobby, a large photograph of Haden displayed his senior picture with his beaming smile, compassionate eyes, and dark hair like mine. A slideshow of memories played on either side. Haden had a gentle demeanor that

---

1. Jennifer L. Betts, "Understanding and Healing Through 30 Suicide Awareness Quotes," *Love to Know*, February 10, 2025, 1.

made everyone feel peaceful around him, and the photos revealed that in many varied ways.

Bobby shifted from one foot to the other. "One time in the gym, he asked me to pray for him. Then he kept going on afterward about how much it meant to him. But it was me that it meant so much to. That was Haden's way of bringing me out and getting me closer to God. I'll forever be thankful for him. He will always be in my heart. I love you, Haden."

As I listened, I couldn't help but smile through my tears, because it was true: whether in the park, at the grocery store, or the vet's office—wherever Haden was—he wasn't ashamed to share God's love for people through prayer. In that moment, one treasured memory came to mind. Haden had told me he was in the local hardware store one day when he felt God leading him to pray for an older man. He went over and asked if he could pray for him. The man replied, "Well, I'm an atheist, but if you think you need to pray, go ahead," and Haden *did* pray for that man. Of course, I wondered if that planted any seeds of faith in that man's heart. Sometime later, I had an amazing thought—when I get to Heaven, I might just get to meet the atheist from the hardware store.

Among the many who spoke that day were Haden's most recent youth pastors, Kyle and Megan, who were husband and wife. Kyle stepped up first, calm, with his rapid way of speaking. He said, "If you knew Haden, you knew two things: He loved God, and he loved people. When we first got up here, I'd never been a youth pastor before, and I had this nervous tic when I would speak, and I'd turn my head to the side and cough a couple times. And I did it all the time. And one night, I see Haden get up and leave, which is weird for Haden because he's not that kid who's gonna get up and walk out. So, I just kept going. And he comes back and sits in the front row, and he had a cough drop in his hand, trying to secretly pass it off to me."

Everyone laughed, and miraculously, a chuckle even escaped my lips. That was *so* Haden.

Kyle went on to share how Haden would boldly share his faith. As his youth pastor, Kyle admitted that he looked up to Haden when

Haden should have been looking up to him. "If I can say anything at all, I want my sons to be just like Haden."

He passed the mic to Megan, a petite young woman with long, dark hair, who came up to her husband's shoulder. She fought to hold back tears as she stepped forward. "I'd like to share a few words to describe Haden. There's so many: *genuine, kind, God-fearing.* He was probably my favorite person to talk about God with because it wouldn't matter what you were talking about, if it had God it in, he was on the edge of his seat and his eyes would light up and the smile on his face, and you could just tell by looking at him that he wanted to soak up as much as he could and he couldn't wait to pour it back out." She choked back the overwhelming emotions we were all experiencing. "He inspired me so much, 'cause he made me want to go after God harder. He taught us so much." A lightheartedness took over her tone. "I always got along with Haden, but I had one argument with him. One afternoon, he came with some other youth to my house, and while we were sitting around talking, I found him in the kitchen looking for a rag. He insisted on doing my dishes. I told him, 'You aren't doing my dishes, Haden,' but he said, 'I just want to be a blessing to you. I was taught to always leave things better than I found them. You let us come over here for lunch, and I just want to give back to you.' Needless to say, he won that argument."

After hearing those heartfelt memories, our whole family moved to the stage for support and reassurance, from Haden's forty-eight-year-old dad to his twelve-year-old little brother. I swallowed fear like an unchewed piece of steak. I was to be the first to speak. I wanted nothing more than to run and hide, but I stood proud and spoke strongly to honor my son, followed by my husband in like manner.

Next, my twenty-one-year-old daughter, Brittany, stepped forward. I stood on one side of her, her husband, Caleb, on the other. Her long blonde hair framed a face of beauty and sorrow as she struggled through the words she'd written.

I handed her tissues, put a hand on her back, and stared down at the podium, praying for strength for my daughter.

"Nothing in life is perfect, but Haden, you sure were the closest thing to perfect," she said. "I'm so thankful God placed you in my life to be my little brother because He knew that I would need you. You were—you are—my first best friend forever. Most siblings don't have the relationship we have had. You were—and you are—the most forgiving, caring, and loving person I have ever met. And I always thought to myself, *Man, I hope one day I marry someone just like my brother.* I don't think that's something I ever shared with you, Bub. It was amazing to see how you would put so much time and effort into things because they were important to you. The last time I went deer hunting, you were with me, and I shot a small buck, but you were so excited and felt so privileged just to watch me experience something you love doing so much. I loved sharing that with you. You were the hardest worker, the best guitar player, the best researcher, the best Christian, lover of Christ, best friend, son, and brother there ever has been. Gosh, I just love you so much. Until we meet again. Love, your *favorite* sister." The crowd chuckled at the emphasized word.

Finally, our son, Dylan, who was only twelve at the time, took his turn. With sandy blonde hair and a black, button-up shirt, he stepped up to the mic and started emphatically, "Me and Haden were bad, bad boys!" The whole audience burst out in laughter. Dylan went on to tell how he and his brother occasionally went on fun little outings on Haden's dirt bike (when Mom left the house, of course). "We would sneak out and go riding beside the highway and down to the boat docks. We would go to these hundred-foot cliffs that were inside a surrounded bay. It was really tall rocks that were really beautiful. It was really pretty when the water was calm and really quiet. And on Friday nights we would go riding into town in his loud truck. He would be beating on his steering wheel, jamming out, and it would get kinda scary 'cause he would be looking down at the ground half the time. But he would take me out to eat and huntin' for chicks. I think he would take me with him so he could get more attention, 'cause I'm so cute and all. Then we'd go back to his house, and I would help him clean his house, and we would play video games, and he would play his guitar, and he'd show me his bow and arrow and all the new things he learned about it. But I loved him, and he was the best bro in the world."

The entire eulogy was carried out by about twenty people—Haden's whole family along with many extended family members, friends, and pastors. We were solid and steadfast in our purpose to celebrate our son, brother, cousin, grandson, and friend for the beautiful life he lived, sharing stories of Haden, laughing together at funny happenings that involved him, and reminiscing over the beautiful heart this young man possessed. We wanted a celebration of life not only to thank Haden for being our son but to thank God for giving him to us and to thank those who had loved our son and touched his life in so many ways.

Before we'd arrived for the memorial, I hadn't been sure I could face this day. As our vehicle had slowed for the last turn into the church parking lot, I sucked in air, preparing to face one of the hardest moments of my life. To say I was overwhelmed was an understatement. I felt I would explode at any moment from the potent ball of emotions that bombarded my soul. *No, hold it together! To honor your son!* But as the vehicle slowed, and I saw the parking lot packed out in the middle of the COVID-19 pandemic, the strangest feeling of joy hit me in the midst of my debilitating sorrow. It was such a weird emotion for the occasion. But that momentary joy came when I saw how much my son was loved. How much my son mattered! How much we mattered! We greatly appreciated the love and honor shown to him that day. No one walked away from the gathering without seeing the value in this young man's life, and that, although his life was short, it was also powerful and effective for Christ.

Our daughter's best friend, Alyssa, had flown in to stay with us. She came not only to support our daughter but also to share in word and song with her at the celebration of life, for someone she considered like a little brother. The following day, on her flight back to California, Alyssa texted me, sharing, "I've never been a part of something so incredibly beautiful that was intended to be so incredibly ugly. God has much to teach us, and it is evident your ears are wide open to hear from Him, even in as hard of a time as this. I've never been more inspired to have faith in our Father. Thank you."

The Day When Hell Came to Visit

It was a normal, quiet Sunday afternoon, the kind that held full hearts, full bellies, and afternoon naps that flowed from a morning of worship, fellowship, and food. Our daughter and son-in-law had been at church, but our oldest son, Haden, hadn't made it that day, which was unusual for him. I assumed it was because he had been sick that week. So, although I called and didn't get an answer from him, we went about our normal routine of church, then lunch, then home. We had gone upstairs to settle in and watch a TV series while our youngest son, Dylan, played games in his room nearby. I ran downstairs to slip into some warm, fuzzy pajamas. As I walked into my room, I heard a phone ring and my husband's voice mumbling something in an urgent tone, then a commotion upstairs. It alarmed me. Then, almost immediately, my cell phone rang, and I thought, *That's weird—who is calling?*

Before I could say hello, our daughter, Brittany, yelled through the phone, "Mom, come now!" Her voice trembled with quick, shallow breaths. The call to my husband must have also been from her. She didn't stay on the line to explain but just blurted out again, "Come now!" before hanging up. I stood frozen and confused, trying to figure out what was happening and what she meant. I heard my husband from upstairs—screaming, blubbering—then the sound of feet pounding quickly across the floor and more commotion. My chest tightened while a lump in my throat threatened to choke me.

I ran to the hallway just as my husband rounded the corner at the bottom of the stairs. He yelled out in dread, "It's Haden, let's go!" He didn't elaborate, and I was too scared to ask. My entire body shook as I grabbed my purse and phone, and nothing more than a whimper escaped my trembling lips.

When you hear a tone from your spouse's voice—pure and sheer horror—unlike anything you've ever heard in the twenty-six years of your marriage, you instantly know this day is going to be beyond anything you've ever suffered.

Terror gripped my heart, and it was as if someone pressed play, flooding my mind with the worst imaginable scenarios, though none came close to the devastating truth I was about to face. My husband

Robert, my son Dylan, and I grabbed our shoes and flew to the car. We were headed to our daughter's property, where Haden lived in a tiny home. My mother happened to live next door to them both.

In the car, crying, praying aloud, and pleading with God were full-on. Our youngest, twelve at the time, sat in the back seat with a flat gaze and dull eyes. My husband gripped the steering wheel hard as he flattened the pedal to the floor. It was as if everything was happening so fast, but it was all in slow motion at the same time. Just as we rounded the top of the last hill, we saw an ambulance with lights flashing and sirens blaring cresting over the hill opposite us. This sight gutted me and brought more intense wailing and prayer. We turned left, speeding down the road to our son Haden's house, and saw our daughter and her husband standing outside with Grandma and an aunt and cousin who had been visiting my mom at the time.

I was so confused. I knew our son had been sick, but it was just a cold, maybe even COVID. But he had told us the day before that he was feeling better, and he was going to run to town for some errands. But this day, we arrived in his yard with cops filing out of his house and a stretcher lying unused in the doorway. I was bewildered, knowing something was very wrong with my son but believing that we would get to see him. We would get to talk to him and tell him how much we loved him. I knew he had been sick, but never did I imagine it was this tragic.

When our tires screeched to a halt, I stumbled out of the car, clutching my jacket and phone. My husband held back near the car. I didn't understand or even process why. I hurried up to my family standing in the yard, some crying, some holding each other, and others with a distant, cloudy gaze.

My brow furrowed, and my mouth stood open. I fumbled, "W—well... what's wrong?" A sharp breath escaped—I hadn't realized I'd been holding it. My chest tightened as I forced out the words, "What happened? I...I... don't understand. Is he still sick?"

Everyone paused, looking at me. Then my mother came over, grabbed me by the forearms, and shook me. "He's dead!"

I stepped back, screamed, and threw my jacket and phone to the ground. I turned away and collapsed to my knees! I felt sure the full contents of my stomach would be on the ground at any second. But the next small block of time is gone—I don't remember it—but my daughter says she watched as my whole body flailed up and down on the ground. I can't recall it. I just know I immediately wanted to die. My worst nightmare!

Life stopped.

It felt like the doors of hell had been flung wide open.

And I was shoved inside for a guided tour.

My first encounter with pure hell.

My heart was ripped out and thrown down on the lawn that day, and I knew life would never be the same. In all honesty, that ache, that terror, cannot truly be put into words.

I don't remember what was said about the particulars of my son's death after that. Everything immediately blurred. I'm sure I went into shock the second I heard the words, "He's dead!"

The rest of our immediate family and myself were likely in shock for well over the first month. We would catch ourselves staring off into space, knowing at any minute we would wake up from this alternate reality into a reality where the world was right again. But it didn't happen. It's appalling how, even a year later, the first thought that still runs through your mind when you wake is, *Is this real? Is my son really dead? Please let it be a nightmare!* It's bewildering how, years down the road, thinking back to the particulars can cause sheer terror to come flooding back to your heart.

OUR AMAZING SON AND BROTHER

Haden was an amazing young man. He had turned twenty the month before we lost him. I say "lost," but I've heard the word *lost* used when you don't know where something is. We know right where our boy is. He isn't lost but in Heaven, with no more tears, no more pain, and no more loneliness or confusion.

Our son was a fine young man, extremely handsome and smart. He had a tender heart and bear hugs he loved to share. As you saw from his celebration of life, I don't think anyone who knew him would disagree when I say he was a young man after God's own heart. He grew up with his older sister and younger brother in church and was given a Christian education. He was on the worship team for several years, and although learning the guitar was a struggle for him, he gave his whole heart to it because he saw it as a way to glorify God. He was an unashamed worshiper. He was never afraid to be who he was and never seemed to think of himself as better than anyone else. Haden always seemed happy or goofy. He was good at researching any topic that interested him. He was saving himself for marriage and had never tried alcohol or drugs. He had just started teaching Royal Rangers on Wednesday nights at church, a young boys' ministry he'd grown up in. He had just gotten his dream truck and had been living out on his own for about four months. Before that, he'd spent ten months with his sister and brother-in-law working toward his independence. He had a good job working as a heavy machine operator and was very good at what he did. He was working his way up the ranks in his dad's excavating business, preparing to take over one day. He was an avid hunter. He had started learning taxidermy and videography on the side, with hopes of starting a social media channel on hunting. Haden loved hanging out with family and friends and attended every youth function he could. Essentially, Haden was the son and brother *any* family would want.

FROM THE MOUNTAINTOP TO THE PITS OF HELL

Our family began in 1992, when Robert and I met, fell madly in love, and married two years later. At the time of the tragedy, we had been together for twenty-eight years and married for twenty-six. I was a stay-at-home mom, homeschooled our kiddos, and worked as the secretary for our family businesses. I didn't become a homemaker because I had no other aspirations in life. I became a homemaker because I knew it was the most important endeavor I could ever hope to accomplish. My husband was an entrepreneur who built multiple reputable, thriving businesses from scratch. He had always dreamed of growing up, getting married, having kids, and working hard enough to accomplish the task of allowing his wife to stay at home with his kids, and he satisfied that dream.

We weren't perfect by any means. We still had our struggles in life. A successful family doesn't just happen by chance without sacrifice, hard times, and mistakes. Neither of us grew up in a Christian home. Although we didn't start our marriage as Christians, we quickly saw the need to have a higher power helping to raise our family. All our children were brought up in a Christian home. We were highly involved in the church throughout our walk with the Lord. Over the years, I taught Sunday school and served in drama ministry, women's ministry, youth ministry, nursery, and children's ministry. My husband served in the bus ministry, taught Sunday school, and was a deacon for years. Still, this service and loyalty to the Lord didn't guarantee physical protection, which is one of the hardest lessons we've had to learn. Even if your family is walking with the Lord, praying and believing in faith for His protection, this kind of tragedy can still happen.

Further, we didn't suffer from absent-parent syndrome. My husband and I focused on raising our kids to be God-fearing, hardworking, and family-oriented. We were emotionally available parents. We set limits and defined responsibilities and expectations for our children. My husband and I poured our lives into raising our children, giving them what we didn't have as kids, more than just the material things. We wanted a family that wasn't ravaged by divorce or the waywardness of the world. We gave blood, sweat, tears, and a whole lot of prayers in raising each of our children. And just when we thought we would be transitioning to a new level of lessened commitment, it hit us—our son needed us more than he ever had before.

It's inconceivable to see your child gone so soon, just when his adult life was beginning. We felt like we'd poured our lives into this young man over the past twenty years, and it was all for naught. Not that we didn't love the years we were given. Not that those years weren't effective for the Lord. It just seemed like everything we had worked so hard for utterly vanished in an instant. Haden had so much potential we would never see fulfilled. It didn't seem fair, and it surely wasn't natural.

Essentially, life was beautiful until that day when we found ourselves in the deepest valley. Forget the valley—we found ourselves deep in the undermost trenches of hell. Never in our wildest nightmares would we have guessed we'd find ourselves here. Yet, sadly, we were unknowingly very acquainted with what brought on this tragedy.

FAMILY HISTORY OF DEPRESSION

My husband, Robert, had struggled with mild to moderate depression throughout his life, but he knew his feelings didn't match his reality. I would talk to him, love him, and reason with him, which I've since learned may help with some types of depression, but for cases of major depression (like Haden likely suffered), encouragement alone is not enough.

Since my husband and I had already walked through his own bouts of depression for more than twenty-eight years, the few times when my son voiced his struggles with depression during his teen years, we weren't as highly alarmed as we should have been. And although medical intervention was spoken of, Robert and Haden both voiced they wanted nothing to do with medication. I later found this is common in those who suffer from depression for a variety of reasons— whether it's the stigma of being "on medication," a desire to avoid anything unnatural or potentially addictive, or, for believers, trusting God would heal them if it was His will.

Both Robert and Haden assured me they would be okay. I believed they understood themselves enough to know when they would need something more. I've never regretted something more in my life. And I've come to learn humans can't understand themselves or their own needs when in depression because depression, unlike other physical illnesses in the body, literally affects your thinking. "It can impair your attention and memory, as well as your information processing and decision-making skills."[2] Let me reiterate, it is dangerous to assume someone who is depressed will be self-aware enough to know when to get help. We later came to understand that each person's depression can be profoundly different and that there are all different types of

---

2. James Cartreine, "More Than Sad: Depression Affects Your Ability to Think," Harvard Health Blog, May 6, 2016, 1, https://www.health.harvard.edu/blog/sad-depres sion-affects-ability-think-201605069551.

depression with different depths, different ignition switches, and different, often complex needs for healing. Heartbreakingly, on that tragic day, we found out that major depression is no respecter of persons, no respecter of faith, and no respecter of reason.

CHRISTIANS DON'T GET DEPRESSED

When you hear about someone who suffers from major depression, many images and notions may come to mind, likely because there are many *false* assumptions and stigmas associated with depression, such as: Christians don't get depressed. Happy people don't get depressed. Only ungrateful people get depressed. Only selfish people get depressed. Your faith is weak if you're depressed. Only individuals who are unmotivated or lazy get depressed. Or, depressed people aren't mentally strong.

In all honesty, I had my assumptions about what a person with depression was like, though, ironically, they didn't even fit my husband's character or background. I thought people with depression must have lived through horrible tragedies and traumas, struggled with their looks or weight, or were individuals who felt their lives simply had no glimmer of hope.

Major depression is likely what overtook my son. And honestly, he was not consistent with any of the ideas I'd had about it. He had a blessed life. He had an eternal hope, and he always seemed happy and thankful. He was one of the most grateful people I knew. (He constantly told his dad and me "thank you" for anything and every-thing, even daily meals.) He was not lazy by any means. He worked a full-time job, and he had two side jobs he was working to perfect his skills in videography and taxidermy. And although he had been diag-nosed with dyslexia in his school years, he had overcome most of the issues associated with it, and he was a very profound thinker. (I've also since learned that those with dyslexia suffer a 46 percent higher rate of suicide than those in the average population.[3]) Haden's faith was

---

3. "Working with Governments: Dear Dyslexic Foundation," accessed November 2023, cover page, https://www.deardyslexic.com/working-with-governments.

stronger than almost anyone else's I knew. He was extremely handsome. He was highly motivated and was always out in the woods hunting or hiking. He was working out when he could fit it in. He was always doing things to join in at church and was outgoing and loved being around people. And many would agree he had a solid family life. Most people would not associate these attributes with someone who has depression. By all accounts, he looked like he was savoring life at every turn. Although he wrestled with "the blues" off and on, as my husband also had for twenty-eight years, I never would have thought he was at the point of no return.

As you saw from those who spoke at Haden's celebration of life, having depression can't stop a person from contributing profoundly to their family, their job, and their society. As you already know, my husband also struggles with depression (likely Persistent Depressive Disorder, sometimes called Dysthymia). He has since his teen years, and even though it has been an ongoing illness, he brings tremendous joy, leadership, strength, and stability to our family. Unfortunately, perhaps in part because of the added value that both Robert and Haden brought to our lives while suffering from depression, we *misunderstood* it. We not only misunderstood it, but we were also ignorant of its cunningness, its complexity, and its ability to hide in plain sight.

A GLIMPSE OF THE ENEMY

As I searched for answers, I learned that up to 60 percent of suicide deaths are linked to major depression.[4] Because depression has the potential to be deadly, it's crucial to understand it, recognize it, and treat it as soon as it is discovered. If our family had had an accurate understanding of depression, we may *not* have missed Haden's life-threatening illness and, in turn, might have potentially saved his life.

Often, those suffering from depression see it as a personal failure, not realizing it's a medical condition that needs to be attacked from all

---

4. Leonard Homes, "Suicide Statistics in the United States," *Verywell Mind,* June 24, 2021, https://www.verywellmind.com/suicide-rates-overstated-in-people-with-depression-2330503.

fronts, including through medical care, talk therapy, and spiritual warfare. This is why it is so important for family and friends to recognize the warning signs, speak up, and help their loved one get the care they need.[5] Those suffering from depression often don't understand that no matter how much you berate yourself, you will not be able to just pull yourself out of it. I believe my son struggled in much the same way. After he died, I found a small entry in a journal I had bought him. It read, "Charge: No more negativity! Help yourself—by yourself." This destroyed me when I read it. I believe he had struggled with his depression for a long time, but he didn't realize it was depression; he only saw it as a weakness in himself. If there were better awareness and fewer stigmas regarding mental health, this might not have been the case. Haden didn't understand what was happening to him and how deadly this disease could become.

There may be many reasons why someone never gets care for depression, whether due to financial difficulties, a lack of awareness, or even their own reluctance to respond to what they're feeling. Whatever the reasons, the longer depression goes untreated, the worse it can become.

Because depression is difficult to detect, it is no wonder that this devious disease can easily be misread and mismanaged, especially when those who suffer from it often try to conceal it. People who are depressed often deny, misidentify, or completely miss their symptoms. For our family and friends, it was incomprehensible—inconceivable— to discover that our son was so severely depressed that he died from suicide.

WHY DIDN'T WE SEE THIS COMING?

Unfortunately, this is the first question you ask yourself if you've lost a loved one this way—and the question that continues to haunt you thereafter. Depression is not always obvious to family, friends, or even

---

5. Detailed explanations about depression are beyond the scope of this book. So for those that want more information on depression, I have bonus material on my website regarding depression and recommended resources in the appendix of this book.

the person suffering. Diagnosing depression isn't easy, even for professionals. Those suffering are often able to function somewhat normally, even though they have a major battle taking place inside them. They often don't let others in on it because they feel it is just a personal weakness or something they need to "figure out" on their own. We didn't fully understand or see what was happening to Haden, so I highly doubt he understood it either. In my layman's research, I've learned this is true for many people who find themselves in the depths of depression. They are in the middle of it and don't even know what is happening to them.

There are also a lot of myths or misinformation about depression symptoms. The average person assumes (likely because it's what we commonly hear) that all depressed people feel sad or want to sleep all day. While this is true for some, this is not true for everyone. For a large number of people, depression expresses itself as irritability, guilt, worthlessness, or a feeling of "being trapped." Many depression sufferers have a hard time sleeping at all, lying awake for hours on end while the irritability, hopelessness, or guilt preys on them throughout the night.

One form of depression is called high-functioning depression or smiling depression. Individuals with this form of depression appear happy and are often the overachievers who work and give so much, yet they are, in essence, *running* from their depression, likely because it is in the quiet, "calm" times that the depression makes itself known.

Only in hindsight did we discern the signs that our son had been headed into major depression. Only after his passing did we put it all together. He had been pulling away from friends, family, and some of his normal activities, a common sign of major depression. At the time, I guess we figured this was all just part of normal growing up and becoming his own man. He was at a transitional period in his life, so we were at a loss to detect anything "out of the normal," since we didn't even know what his new "normal" was. (Parents! Please stay alert during times of transition for your adult children. This time can hide issues well.)

Haden had a very tender heart, and we believe his depression intensified because of the loss of loved ones our family endured that year, along with the fact that he was, for the first time, living on his own. Only later did I learn that living alone is like taking poison to a depressed person. In addition, a major trigger for depression (mild to chronic) is the loss of a loved one. Of course, the fear and isolation of COVID-19, the bitter winter, and the political and global chaos of 2020 only added to the weight he was carrying. I believe young and old alike looked at the future through a very dirty window at that point. I'm sure Haden, like a lot of young people, had lost hope that their future would look anything like their parents' lives.

AN ALL-TOO-COMMON PROBLEM

You have probably heard of Rick Warren, the famous pastor of Saddle-back Church, a megachurch with campuses around the world. He is one of the most influential, evangelical Christian pastors in the United States and the famous author of *The Purpose Driven Life,* which has been translated into more languages than any other book aside from the Bible. But what you may *not* know is that the Warrens also had a son who suffered from depression most of his life. According to the Warrens, their son's siblings had even "talked him off the ledge many times." When the Warrens found out about his illness, they were able to get their son the best doctors in the world, the best medications, and the best spiritual guidance and counseling possible. But even with their knowledge and all the help and prayers they could have mustered, sadly, their son still took his own life. He was twenty-seven years old at the time. Rick Warren has now become a major advocate for brain health and is on a mission to abolish the stigma associated with brain health issues. Rick Warren says, "People who take their own life don't really want to die; they just want to end the pain."[6]

I believe this was true for my son. He didn't want to die. He just wanted to end the pain. I don't believe my son chose (in the normal manner of "making choices") to take his own life. If you knew Haden personally, you would understand the truth of that statement. The last

6. YouTube, "Rick Warren Testimony."

thing he would ever want to do was hurt someone. He loved life, the Lord, and others too much to choose this end.

HIS LIFE AND HIS LEGACY

As you have read our story, I hope that it has given you a deeper understanding of my son's character. More importantly, I hope it has shown you that the *value* of Haden's life far outweighed the way his life ended. Greater still, I pray that you, at some point, can see how the beauty of your own loved one's life surpasses the way they left this world. I pray that through this book and my son's story, you find healing. Even greater, I pray you find hope.

I want to share one last memory with you. The day after Haden's celebration of life, my dear friend Megan, Haden's youth pastor, sent me a text. She shared this: "Friend, when I spoke about Haden and shared how he was taught to always leave every*thing* better than he found it, I was thinking about how he helped with my dishes that night. But then I realized it was so much more. Haden left every*one* better than he found them."

I believe this is Haden's legacy: though he left this world far sooner than we had ever hoped, he made every life he touched better. My prayer, dear friend, is that his story leaves you better, too.

Dear Lord,

Thank You for helping me see I'm not alone. Thank You for helping me see that others have walked this hellish road before me, yet have survived. Thank You for helping me see that others understand the many trials of losing a loved one in such an unbelievable way. Thank You for helping me see there are people who care about me right now. Lord, help me to read this book with an open heart. Help me to better understand not only where my lost loved one was on that fateful day, but that they, too, deserve to be remembered for so much more than just how their life ended. Lord, help me to see hope at this crushing time because hope feels elusive.

In Jesus's name, amen.

CHAPTER 2

SPIRITUAL TRAUMA

WRESTLING WITH GOD

Until you've wrestled with God, you'll never know the depth of His love.
The power of His hand. Or the grace of His heart.
—Daniel Goldstein

Oftentimes, people nonchalantly look at our lives as Christians to see how we live, but they bring out the magnifying glass when tragedy strikes. Why is that? Likely because it is in the hardship of life that true faith is revealed and superficial faith is unmasked. We never know which one will play out in our lives. What follows in this chapter is not a definitive map of a spiritual process, but rather my story, which I pray helps you see you are not alone if you, too, suffer from a crisis in your faith. The journey through grief is different for everyone, and your path may differ significantly from mine, and that's okay. You may not even experience a crisis in your faith, but for those who do experience this spiritual trauma and are wrestling with God, be assured, this is often a normal part of grief.

FUNCTIONING ON SHOCK AND CHRISTIAN AUTOPILOT

We had so many people at Haden's celebration of life who voiced that they were inspired by the way we were able to function in the aftermath of such a tragedy. But there were many days afterward when they might not have been so inspired.

Our full intent that day was to honor our son and the beautiful life he had lived. We likely only accomplished what we did because we were in shock, gripped by the trauma that usually accompanies this type of loss, and running on what I call Christian autopilot—functioning as we had always known to function, in line with God's Word. We were doing all we could to not only honor the God who had always stood beside us but to honor the son He had blessed us with. But as the shock wore off and the fog began to clear, I started to grasp our situation all too clearly. And what I began to see did not sit well with me.

GOD, WHERE ARE YOU?

After such a terrible loss, I needed God more than ever, but He seemed so far away. It felt like a literal barrier separated us. I tried to pray, but no words would come. I tried to read His Word, but there was no feeling, no revelation. I tried to worship, but I was numb. *Where are You, God?* For months and months after my son's passing, it seemed almost impossible to focus on any type of prayer, Bible reading, or worship. Honestly, I had little desire to do any of it.

Only later did I notice that this was a common occurrence in the Bible with people who were in great trial or despair. King David shares in Psalm 10:1, "O, LORD, why do you stand so far away? Why do you hide when I am in trouble?" Job explains it this way: "I go east, but he is not there. I go west, but I cannot find him. I do not see him in the north, for he is hidden. I look to the south, but he is concealed" (Job 23:8–9). We know Jesus felt the same way as He was dying on the cross. God's one and only Son, the One in whom He was well pleased, the perfect Lamb—He cried out, "My God, my God, why have you abandoned me?" (Matthew 27:46).

Job was a blameless man of complete integrity. King David was called a man after God's own heart. Even God's Son cried out, feeling abandoned.

Left behind?

Deserted?

Even God's anointed and some of the most faithful figures in all of Scripture suffered moments of profound loneliness during their darkest trials. Abandoned by God? But was it true? Does God really leave people when they need Him most?

That question haunted me. It was a scary place, thinking I had lost God's presence... and my peace. At the time, I didn't understand, and that confusion only made me more angry, bitter, and skeptical.

ARE YOU QUESTIONING THE VALIDITY OF GOD'S LOVE?

After our loss, going anywhere was uncomfortable, but church was the worst place for me. It seems strange that the place where we'd normally find the most comfort only brought anxiety. Let me be clear: I have a great church family who are vibrant and led by the Spirit, but what brought this feeling was my situation, not my church. It was far from comforting going there, knowing every person there knew what had happened. It made me feel sick to my stomach. When I wanted my presence to be downplayed more than ever, I felt like I had a spotlight following me with all eyes on me and my family.

I stood in the church each week, with worship songs flashing up on the screen, with words whose validity I couldn't help but question. Week after week, I would go hoping to find comfort, but it seemed I just grew more hardened. Words out of the Scripture reading or to worship songs would come up, and I felt myself growing more and more bitter.

Some songs spoke of God's unfailing faithfulness, promising that He would never let us down. I cringed and thought, *Nope, that isn't true. He completely, utterly, and in the worst way imaginable let me down. That song...is a lie!* Then came the songs declaring God's goodness over and over, but I couldn't bring myself to believe it. *That doesn't feel true either.*

Even when my pastor would confidently say, "God is good... all the time." I would have thoughts like *No pastor, God is not good all the time. And some of the time, God is really, really bad.* When such pain, loss, and fear grip you, I believe it's only natural to wrestle with these thoughts. I was having a problem reconciling a loving God with such torment. Just realize these feelings are normal and God *can* handle them.

WHEN YOU FEEL TORN IN TWO

It felt like I had become two different people. One version of me still had a relationship with God—still trusted Him, mainly because my belief in Him and His Word had been so deeply woven into my life. I had borne witness to the power of Christ firsthand, and I couldn't deny His existence or His presence.

But there was another version of me—the part that couldn't seem to find the way back to God. A wall stood between us, built with one painful glaring question: *WHY DID YOU ALLOW THIS TO HAPPEN!* And there was no satisfying answer.

Yet something kept telling me that God was the answer. I began to see I had *not* lost my loyalty, obedience to, or belief in God, but I felt I had lost my *joy* and *love* for Him. It was a strange place to be.

The Scriptures made it clear that if we deliberately turn from God, we are cutting ourselves off from God's forgiveness. To be called by His name, we must persevere even in trials.[1] Something kept telling me, *Just keep walking toward God.* Somehow, I continued to walk toward Him, even with bitterness as my walking partner.

ARE YOU FINDING FAITH BUT NOT JOY?

One day, I questioned God, annoyed. "Hmph, how am I supposed to get my joy in You back?" Later that very day, I was reading from my GriefShare book, and I saw this Scripture from Psalm 16:11 (AMPC),

---

1. Hebrews 6:4–6 (esv) states, "For it is impossible, in the case of those that have once been enlightened, who have tasted the heavenly gift, and have shared in the Holy Spirit, and have tasted the goodness of the word of God and the powers of the age to come, and then have fallen away, to restore them again to repentance, since they are crucifying once again the Son of God to their own harm and holding him up to contempt."

which reads: "You will show me the path of life; in Your presence is fullness of joy; at Your right hand there are pleasures forevermore."

I was taken aback. I had asked the question, and He answered me on the very same day. As I read that first part—"You will show me the path of life"— I saw that God was saying, "I am directing your path." The verse went on to say, "In your presence is fullness of joy." So He told me that if I wanted to find my joy in Him again, I would need to spend time in His presence. The Scripture went on, "At your right hand there are pleasures forevermore." This reiterated to me that if I want to spend eternity in Heaven, I must maintain my relationship with God; He alone holds the keys to eternity.

God gave me the answer to the question of how I was to find joy in Him again, although I didn't know whether I liked the answer. Honestly, I was still a little less than happy with Him. Why would I want to spend time with Him? Why worship Him? At that point, I still wanted, desperately, just to die. Again, I heard, *Just keep walking toward God*. So even though it felt so fruitless, and I felt so resentful, I walked toward Him, begrudgingly. Friend, I know joy likely not only seems far away but it may even feel literally impossible right now, and that is okay. Joy and grief are like oil and water right now. Let me encourage you: just keep walking toward God.

DOING THINGS YOU DON'T NECESSARILY WANT TO DO

I understood I needed to spend more time with God, so I determined within myself I would spend time with Him, no matter how hollow it felt. I read my Bible and prayed daily, even though it felt pointless and I felt empty. One Sunday, I was determined to try to publicly worship God. The day arrived. I swallowed hard and clenched my teeth as I raised my hands to attempt worship. (Before this tragedy, I loved to worship God.) But a time of *thanksgiving* and *praise*? What could I be thankful for? How could I praise Him now, in the middle of the worst tragedy of my life? For the first time in my life, it felt like it was truly a *sacrifice* of praise. The pain of my loss shot through my body. I stumbled and almost collapsed into the chairs in front of me. Then I stood. I stood in my brokenness, loss, and bitterness, not wanting to worship.

But I knew the only way back to God would perhaps *take doing some things I didn't necessarily want to do.*

At that moment, I realized what worship truly was. For the first time, it was as if worship *cost me* something. That worship came out of my little. Out of my "at the end of my rope" worship. Out of my "I don't know if I can go on" worship. Just as God was well pleased with the widow who gave out of her poverty,[2] I believe He cherishes it all the more when we worship in our little, in our pain, in our suffering. I believe it is all the more cherished by the Lord when we worship, even if it hurts to do so. More clearly than ever, I saw that worship was raising God up because that is His deserved place, regardless of my circumstance. I finally understood what a sacrifice of praise felt like. If you haven't already, I would encourage you to try to worship. If you can't even think of doing it publicly, try it in privacy. I would encourage you, in any way you can, to spend time with God.

ARE YOU ANGRY WITH GOD?

The following week, while I was working through my GriefShare workbook, I came to a Scripture that mentions how God knows the number of days each of us has.[3] I knew that verse already, but for some reason, seeing that play out on my son's last day provoked me. According to the GriefShare book, that verse was supposed to bring comfort. Instead, it filled me with rage. Full-blown anger at God!

That's right. He knew! Why would He allow this to happen? He knew the exact day, the exact time, the exact scene, and He knew He would use it for our "good." (My eyes were rolling.) *God knows so much! Well, didn't He know how my son's passing away by a self-inflicted means seemed to me to be the worst possible way he could have died? Didn't God know the pain, suffering, fear, confusion, anger, turmoil, trauma, anxiety, guilt, and utter torment it would put our family through? So, if He knew the exact day he would leave this earth, why couldn't He have had Haden get in a car wreck or have some other unques-*

---

2. "They all gave out of their wealth; but she, out of her poverty, put in everything—all she had to live on" (Mark 12:44 niv).

3. Psalm 139:16 says, "You saw me before I was born. Every day of my life was recorded in your book. Every moment was laid out before a single day had passed."

tionable accident or other critical sickness if this had to be his last day? Why this way? Why such a tragic, questionable, confusing death? Why did He allow Haden to suffer? Why did Haden's mind have to be so tortured with mental illness?

My husband and I just wanted even a few last moments with our son. I agreed wholeheartedly with my husband when he often lamented, "I at least wanted the opportunity to have even understood what our son was going through. So, we could at least have tried to help him." But we didn't get that either. We just wanted the opportunity to tell him how much we loved him and how he had blessed our lives. To tell him he was important and how he would be so dearly missed. But none of us got that. God had to have known how that would torture us! I can only imagine that having the opportunity for your loved one to see that you stood beside them in the battle for their life, even if it was a short time, would be somewhat of a balm for your heart and theirs.

In my anger, I thought I knew what needed to be done. I had to bring God in for an evaluation, one I knew He had already *failed*. He was working for me, and He had disappointed "the boss." And as His "boss," I saw Him as an *incompetent, insubordinate, unethical employee.* How could a tragedy like this happen on His watch?

"GOD... YOU'RE FIRED!"

I yelled, *I don't know if I can love You anymore. Haden would have died for You. How could you let Haden suffer like that alone? How can You allow us to suffer so much without him now? Why would a loving God allow that to happen to us if we were living according to Your Word? If we were bringing Haden up "in the way he should go"? If we had genuine faith in Your protection, how could this happen? Why?*

In my rage, I questioned my pastor and other spiritual leaders in my life. I questioned my counselor, and she assured me Haden wasn't alone and that God had been there with him, but I didn't believe it. In my bitterness and anger, I even thought that was just some Christianese she was spouting at me.

I railed at God. But only as the hot flames of my anger subsided did I realize that just because God knows the day doesn't necessarily mean He chooses how someone passes. God is sovereign, meaning all-powerful, but He is only able to do what is consistent with His character. I'll share more on this questioning of God in subsequent chapters, but for now, know that questioning and anger are normal parts of grief.

Friend, are you angry with God today? If you are, it's okay. Accept your anger. It's part of working through grief. Anger is a natural response to utter confusion and the feeling that we have been lied to. Hold on, I hope to share some things that will lead you to hope. And if we can see hope, even if it is far off, it becomes the lifeline that we can grab onto and slowly pull ourselves out of the pit of grief.

To Truly See God is to Be Truly Changed

Oh, I continued to study God's Word, but it was more likely with the intention of trying to find where God had messed up and where I could call Him out on His utter failure. Only a few days after I had railed so loudly at God, I read this Scripture:

> Where shall I go from your Spirit?
> Or where shall I flee from your presence?
> If I ascend to heaven, you are there!
> If I make my bed in Sheol [hell], you are there!
> If I take the wings of the morning
> and dwell in the uttermost parts of the sea,
> even there your hand shall lead me,
> and your right hand shall hold me.
> If I say, "Surely the darkness shall cover me,
> and the light about me be night,"
> even the darkness is not dark to you;
> the night is bright as the day,
> for darkness is as light with you.
> Psalm 139:7–12 (ESV)

Although it's hard to put this revelation into words, I started to realize something. Maybe there really was no place that my son was beyond God's care and presence. Even as the darkness of Haden's sickness covered him, God was still there with him. There is no place we can be hidden from God; He was there holding Haden even in his darkest hour. Even if Haden couldn't feel it in his sickness, God held him. And even if we couldn't see it in our bitterness, God was holding us.

Part of this Scripture reads, "If I make my bed in Sheol, you are there." (Sheol is the name they used in the Old Testament for hell.) So, even if we, God's followers, find ourselves in the worst possible situations, situations akin to hell, God is still there with us. So...Haden *wasn't* alone in the end. I grabbed onto that verse and claimed it for myself and my son.

It felt as if God leaned in, reassuring me not only of His love for me but also for my son. It was being revealed to me, day by day, more of who God is, but I was also being shown more of who *I* was. I saw that I had believed God was only true and worthy if He met my expectations; otherwise, I deemed Him false and not worthy to follow. Slowly, I realized I had wanted to be the god in my own life; I wanted to be the boss. So, was I making *any* progress? It was all so confusing. And I still had so many questions left unanswered. It seemed I would take one step forward and then two steps back.

Friend, I hope that Scripture spoke to you, as well. I hope you can see that—no matter *what*—your loved one was *not* beyond God's love, care, or presence. Maybe you haven't seen it yet. It may take a lot of wrestling with God to find that place of peace. Keep questioning Him. He isn't afraid of what you'll uncover.

ARE YOU THINKING *WHY BOTHER TO HAVE FAITH?*

All the questions, turmoil, pain, and grief twisted inside of me, and once again, I started to see that you can believe in faith, walking in His will, raise your children in the way they should go, and yet this type of tragedy can *still* happen! I questioned God again, "So why bother to have faith at all if anything can happen to anybody at any time?" Later, as I studied the life of Job, I saw that he too had come to this conclusion in Job 21:15: "Who is the Almighty, and why should we obey him? What good will it do us to pray?"

My thoughts whirled back to my own question: "Why bother to have faith if anything can happen to anybody at any time?" I didn't know if it even made sense, but it felt good to ask it at the time. It seemed like it fit well with my bitter soul. Yet slowly, I realized, it didn't prove my point. Instead, it more clearly spelled out what faith is —because to have faith there must be an unknowing aspect, there must be something we don't understand, a mystery. If we had all the answers, faith would be pointless. God asks us to walk by faith, not by sight, and not by a plan that works out just how *we* want it to. I was essentially equating my life circumstances with God's goodness.

Friend, when we are standing in faith, what we are believing in *may not come to fruition,* but there is a benefit to continuing our walk in faith. At this point, you're likely thinking that benefits are pointless because there doesn't seem to be any benefit that could ever be worth your loss or mine. We would trade *anything* for our lost loved ones. And yet, although nothing will ever suffice for our loss, we must keep moving forward; that's all we can do. We must realize our future holds so much more than this excruciating time of grief. And let me tell you, by experience, it can. If you just keep walking toward God, drawing near to Him, the benefits of walking in faith will soon become more apparent.

ARE YOU USING GOD AS ONLY A MEANS TO GET TO HEAVEN?

I believed in the hope of Heaven. I had hoped for it at that point more than ever. It would be such a joy to go to Heaven, to have eternal life, and to see my son again. In fact, at that point, Robert and I had the same feeling. We wanted nothing more than just to "get" to Heaven. We knew we wanted to see our son again. My husband said it well when he questioned me and several others often with this: "Is it bad that when I get to Heaven, I'll be more excited to see my *son* than God?" Later, as I read *A Grief Observed,* I realized that even C.S. Lewis, the great theologian and Christian apologist, seemed to ponder the same question after the loss of his wife. He wrote in his journal, "Am I, for instance, just sidling back to God because I know if there is any road to H [his deceased wife] it runs through Him?"[4] I worried that I was doing that, as well—using God only as a road to Heaven. A road that led me back to my son. I, too, had the feeling that I wanted so badly to get to Heaven, more to see Haden than to see my Lord.

I believe it's natural to pose that question in the midst of our loss. But I also believe there is a depth of your relationship with God that may currently be in a fog during this time. It's not the most visible thing right now. The pain of your loss is glowing red-hot. Right now, the pain of your loss is louder. Our desire to see our loved ones may be greater right now, and that's okay. Something kept telling me that if I just continued to walk toward God, my love for Him might someday again outshine any human relationship.

WHO IS THIS GOD?

I started to see that I must not really know this God. Who was He? He certainly wasn't the god I had created in my head. That god would have protected my family from such deep pain, that god would have given me not just my needs but my *wants*, that god would not have let my son die! It was obvious I had a lot to work through. I realized I had been creating for myself my own god, one that fit into my box, one that I could understand, one that would never allow anything this hard to come my way.

The more I realized I had made God into someone He is not, the more I wondered if I even loved this new God. I saw God's sovereignty like never before. God is sovereign. Yet, I realized I was measuring God's *goodness* according to my *circumstances*. Just because God is sovereign doesn't mean He chooses or even controls everything that happens in our lives. We must realize there are many outside forces, aside from God, that often play into our trials and tragedies, and because of that, I eventually realized I couldn't blame God.

As I dug more into God's Word, I was learning more about God's true character, and I more clearly saw His plan, which included my *eternal* good. Getting to know God in this way brought greater peace

---

4. C. S. Lewis, *A Grief Observed* (United States: HarperCollins, 2009), 68.

because I realized His plan is good, and His plan ultimately has our best interests at heart. The more I learned of Him, the more I found that I could love Him and trust Him *regardless* of the circumstances of my life.

CAN YOU SEE THE DEPTH OF GOD'S LOVE?

Before this tragedy, I believed God had blessed me with everything in my life, material and nonmaterial. He had blessed me with my husband and all my kids. I believed everything we had belonged to God. And now like never before, I saw that Haden had belonged to God, and God had blessed me with him *for a time*. My view of God was slowly changing. I realized I was blaming God for everything but not giving Him credit for all the good things He had blessed me with. I finally came to the point where I could utter these hard words: "Thank You, God, for blessing me with my son, even if only for a short time!"

Another Scripture I came across in my healing that solidified my belief that God was with us and our son was Romans 8:35–39. Paul asks,

> Can anything ever separate us from Christ's love? Does it mean he no longer loves us if we have trouble or calamity, or are persecuted, or are hungry, or destitute, or in danger, or threatened with death? (As the Scriptures say, "For your sake we are killed every day; we are being slaughtered like sheep.") No, despite all these things, overwhelming victory is ours through Christ, who loved us.
>
> And I am convinced that nothing can ever separate us from God's love. Neither death nor life, neither angels nor demons, neither our fears for today nor our worries about tomorrow—not even the powers of hell can separate us from God's love. No power in the sky above or in the earth below—indeed, nothing in all creation will ever be able to separate us from the love of God that is revealed in Christ Jesus our Lord.

Suffering and pain *were not* just something Paul wrote about; they were his everyday reality. Yet, he endured to the end and won the crown of life that God had promised him. I knew the only way Paul must have endured was because he understood not only God's plan but the depth of God's love, and *I* finally started to see the depth of God's love, as well.

When I asked what this verse meant in regard to my son, this is what I perceived:

Did it mean Christ didn't love Haden because he had trouble and calamity? Did it mean Christ didn't love my son because he was confused in his mind? Sick?

No!

Hallelujah!

No!

Despite all these things, Christ loved Haden. Despite all these things, Haden had an overwhelming victory through his Savior. *Nothing* separated Haden from the love of his Savior. Death didn't separate him from the love of God. The demons, no matter how hard they tried in his trial to confuse Haden's mind, could not separate him from the love of God. Haden's fears on that day didn't separate him from God's love. Even all the powers of hell couldn't keep God's love away from my son. When Haden passed on, he was walking in the light, even if he was sick and confused. He loved his Lord, and his Lord loved him! And he was not separated from that love, not for one second.

One of the best books I've read regarding my faith is titled *"If God Is So Good, Why Do I Hurt So Bad?"* by Dr. David Biebel, a doctor of ministry. As he shared what is most important to God, he wrote, "Jesus wants you whole, whether or not you are well. Whether or not you are well is his concern too, but only a temporary issue. Wholeness has value for this present life *and* for the life to come."[5] This made me realize that although my son Haden was likely not well physically, he was indeed whole spiritually, and *that* was God's greatest concern for him. This is God's greatest concern for us all. He knows that in this life there will be much trial, pain, sickness, and even death and loss,

---

5.   David B. Biebel, *If God Is So Good, Why Do I Hurt So Bad?*, (Orlando, FL: Healthy Life Press, 2014), 96.

and we may have to suffer, but His greatest concern is our eternal wholeness.

I had so many questions about *why*, about suffering, about God's plan, about my perspective versus His perspective, and about eternity, and God walked me through them all. Now that doesn't mean I liked all the answers or that I even received all the answers, but it means I came to fully trust His plan, and I came to fully see His love even in the greatest tragedy of my life. This deeper questioning and doubting helped me to grow stronger in the reason for my hope.

And I finally figured out that something that kept telling me to *just keep walking toward God*, that something that brought God's goodness to my remembrance, that something that was teaching me a new revelation of the Scriptures, that something that was revealing more of God and more of myself, that something that comforted me along the way. It wasn't something, but Someone—the Holy Spirit. John 14:26 shares a little bit about Him: "But when the Father sends the Advocate [Comforter] as my representative—that is, the Holy Spirit—he will teach you everything and will remind you of everything I have told you." Only in hindsight did I realize I was hearing and being led by the Holy Spirit the whole time. He was directing me back to God. He had a front-row seat to my pain and confusion, and He knew that if I could only make my way back to God, I would make it. And He was right. It was so sad that I only recognized Him in hindsight. This was the most beautiful revelation of the Holy Spirit at work in me that I had ever experienced. I had never recognized His work in my life to this degree, and I had to thank Him for all He had done. Although it felt like God was so far away, the Holy Spirit was quite near, and He was pursuing me and urging me toward Himself, all the while empowering me through understanding and peace. What a Comforter, Counselor, Advocate, and Friend!

SO, WHERE WAS GOD?

So, where was God in all of this? He was right there all along. But the pain of my grief was blinding me from seeing Him. It took perseverance not only in my faith but in my grief work to see Him fully again, to trust that He had been by my side all along.

So, friend, I do encourage you to wrestle it out with God. Question God. He is not afraid of what you will find. And I have no doubt, as you work your way through grief and wrestle with God along the way, the Holy Spirit will be there encouraging you, comforting you, teaching you, bringing to your remembrance the goodness of God, and of course reminding you to *just keep walking toward God.*

Like Job, David, the many psalmists in the Bible, and myself, who railed at and wrestled with God, you may be feeling intense anger toward God—but this will slowly pass. As you draw near to Him, He will draw near to you, and you will start to realize a renewed confidence in God's faithfulness and even more in His love for you.

It sounds strange to give you the advice to "wrestle it out with God." If we think about that wrestling match, there is no competition, right? We know who would win. But I think we have to come to that place. The place of seeing that *we* have no comparison to God. But for some peculiar reason, God will bless you with His presence when you wrestle it out with Him. This may be the closest we get to seeing God face to face on this side of Heaven. Not that pain is the only avenue to this depth of a relationship with God, but it's often the only avenue that pries us from our apathy. And that explains why in trial and tragedy, we often grow deeper in our faith than ever. I think it has to do with coming to the end of ourselves and seeing how truly big God is. How great He is. And how there is comfort in that, peace in that, and hope in that.

I don't believe I would have survived had God not been there with me along the way. I made it through because I fully saw the depth of God's love—partly by His not giving up on me, but even more in His not giving up on my son. One point I want people to understand is that I didn't make it through this tragedy because of who *I* am. I made it through because of who *He* is!

Friend, my prayer is that you, too, will find the same hope and peace in God—the Master of Reconstruction.

Dear God,

I guess I don't know You like I thought I did. I'm starting to see that maybe I have lied to myself about who You are. I know I have hope in eternity and hope to see my lost loved one again, but I need to know that is not the only reason that I continue to follow You. I need to know that, and I think You want to know that, as well. I'm still so confused, angry, frustrated, and destroyed. I don't understand this pain, God. People keep telling me this utter devastation will subside, and although that's hard to imagine right now, I will keep walking toward You. I trust You.

In Jesus's name, amen.

CHAPTER 3

THE ULTIMATE QUESTION

WHY IT'S OKAY TO ASK WHY

You may trust the Lord too little, but you can never trust Him too much.
—Hudson Taylor

I f you could ask God one question, my guess is it would line up perfectly with a Barna Poll[1] on the number one question people would want to ask God: "Why does He allow pain and suffering in this world?" When we are grappling with the loss of someone to suicide, this question runs wild through our hearts and minds. In this chapter, I'd like you to see not only why it's okay to ask this question but also how it can help you process your healing journey.

The problem isn't that there are *no answers* to God's purpose or reasoning. The problem? We don't *like* the answers we get. Why? None of us believes our pain is worth the reasons given. We see things merely from a human point of view, not from God's point of view. "Now we see things imperfectly, like puzzling reflections in a mirror, but then we will see everything with perfect clarity. All that I know

---

1. "Top Question People Want to Ask God: Why Allow Pain and Suffering in This World?" *Christian Today*, Accessed March 15, 2023, www.christiantoday.com.au/news/top-question-people-want-to-ask-god-why-allow-pain-and-suffering-in-this-world.html.

now is partial and incomplete, but then I will know everything completely, just as God now knows me completely" (1 Corinthians 13:12). When we see only from our point of view and discount God's eternal plan in our lives, the eternal story of our lives, it's easy to get disillusioned and disgruntled, and potentially walk away from our faith.

We don't like that a loving God permits, allows, or even uses suffering to accomplish His ultimate plan. In fact, we hate that idea so much that we try very hard to deny it to the point of even denying a God who would allow it. Let's remember two important things regarding this. First, we must remember that God is sovereign over all things,[2] meaning He is the supreme ruler. He doesn't run behind Satan, trying to fix things; He already knows what is coming. Second, we must realize that the very heart of God's overall plan involves a loving relationship with us and the ultimate defeat of evil and suffering once and for all. We may not like this two-step process—first this world and then eternity—but this process holds purpose. This time on earth, as hard as it may be, is part of His plan.

WHY IT'S OKAY TO QUESTION GOD IN OUR TRIALS

In grief and suffering, we may have the tenacity in our anger and bitterness to dig into God's Word because we want Him to answer for what He has, at the very least, *allowed* into our lives.

Perhaps you're afraid to question God about your suffering or someone else's. Perhaps you're worried that we aren't allowed to do so. But questions usually lead the way to answers. Let me reiterate, God isn't against us asking questions; He made us inquisitive for a reason. But instead of blaming Him and growing bitter in those questions, God would have us come to the end of ourselves and see that we have no answers within ourselves. At some point, our logic ends. We then naturally must look outside of ourselves. We may look to the world. If so, we may look, study, read, and research, and yet again, we hit a brick wall. We will find no answers of lasting value there, either. In our everyday lives, we don't always think about all that is out of our hands,

---

2. Proverbs 16:33; Isaiah 45:7–9; Colossians 1:16–17; etc.

out of our control, out of our understanding, but when we are faced with a trial that terrifies us so deeply, then we clearly see the depth of these areas of "no control." We realize how small we are and how big God must be.

It only takes a few minutes in the book of Psalms to see that David, a man after God's own heart, questioned God and his suffering—often. And Job, a man who, in God's words, was "blameless, a man of complete integrity," also questioned God. I believe that questioning God may even be part of the process through trial and part of the restoration that follows suffering.

My questioning revealed my weakness; in many ways, I was helpless and at the mercy of everything, but when I leaned into and relied on God, I found a place of peace and safety that was bigger than myself, and therefore, I naturally became stronger. I gained confidence even at my weakest, because I realized my strength was nothing compared to His.

WHERE DID DEATH, TRIALS, AND SUFFERING COME FROM?

Evil, suffering, and death come in many forms, but the two main perpetrators include this cursed world, which came about by way of our sin, and our very real enemy, Satan. In the beginning, when God created everything, He declared it to be good. But God, our Creator, desired a relationship with us. He offered a love relationship with Him, but for the love to be genuine, it had to come through a free choice. Authentic love can't exist without free choice. Unfortunately, God couldn't give us free choice without the potential for evil to exist. As free agents, the humans' choice to rebel opened the door for evil to enter (see Romans 5:12). We should be glad God has given us the freedom of choice. God could take away all evil, but if He did that, He would also have to take away any opportunity for free choice in this world.

In God's plan, our relief from pain, trials, and death will one day be eradicated, but for now, we still live in this cursed world, and we will still have trials on this earth. God has revealed this to us in many ways through His Word, and He also makes it clear that this suffering is temporary. He assures believers that He will be with us through it all.

MAJOR AVENUES OF SUFFERING

Likely somewhere in your grief, you'll ask yourself, "Where do trials and pain come from anyway?" The following are the primary causes of our suffering.

- the curse that made the world imperfect in many ways (sickness, etc.)
- an enemy we have working against us (Satan)
- our evil desires or our carelessness
- other people's evil desires or carelessness
- God, who sometimes allows trials at times to accomplish His objectives, and for our maturity and development of faith
- avoidable or unavoidable accidents, which can fall under several of these areas above

Of course, the main perpetrator is our adversary, Satan, who prowls around like a roaring lion seeking whom he may devour (see 1 Peter 5:8). Death is not what God wanted for my son or your loved one. While a physical illness may have been part of what happened to our loved ones, it is quite likely that there was a spiritual battle at play, as well. As believers, we understand that we live in a world where battles aren't only seen—in fact, they're more often unseen.

IT'S EASY TO BECOME DISILLUSIONED WITH GOD

One day, as my husband Robert and I lamented over the loss of our son, he questioned, "Aren't they always saying Jesus suffered so that we don't have to? This feels an awful lot like extreme suffering to me!" I agreed wholeheartedly. However, I realized this thought process was actually wrong, and it comes because we become hyper-focused on the blessings of living for the Lord. We are continually fed the idea that

Jesus loves us and that our lives will be blessed if we simply follow the Lord. We are even told what my husband mentioned, that "Jesus suffered so we won't have to." That is true to an extent. Jesus saved us from an *eternity* of suffering, but that doesn't mean we won't still suffer in this life. We will all experience pain and suffering on this earth.

Disillusionment occurs when we are disappointed in someone or something that we discover to be less good than we believed. When trials hit us hard, we start to think that God is less good than we had originally believed. Why? In the Christian community, we often hear proclamations like, "My God *will* heal that disease." "My God *will* take care of your debt." "My God *will* cure your sick child." Yet, we know these proclamations aren't always what comes to pass in this world. These proclamations forget a few things, like the free will of human beings, the cursed world we live in, our very real enemy, and the fact that God does, at times, *allow* trials and suffering in our lives.

Don't get me wrong; I'm not saying we shouldn't walk in faith, believing in what we do not see. I'm not saying we shouldn't pray, asking God to deliver us from any trial, sickness, or pain. I'm not even saying we can't change God's mind. These are all biblical truths. However, what I am saying is that if all we ever hear, say, and focus on is how God is going to "fix everything" and we are just going to live blessed lives, we will likely become disillusioned and discouraged. We may potentially walk away from our faith when hardships come.

What is God's *main* mission on the earth? It is to share the good news of salvation and walk beside us every step of the way, not necessarily to heal every person and help His followers avoid every trial or trauma. More than anything, I hope to love, encourage, and strengthen you, but sometimes that means sharing the truth.

Perhaps you thought like I did, *but what about God's promises for protection?* This is an understandable place, partly because of what we are always told about God. In a lot of ways, we harbor a false belief that if we live for the Lord, our lives will always be at ease and we will always be blessed. That God will fix it... He will heal us... He'll send the money... He'll right the wrong. But that doesn't take into account the rest of the Bible, which tells us of trials, tribulations, pain, and suffering that even believers will experience. We must also face the fact that we know perfect outcomes aren't always a reality. In John 16:33, Jesus tells us, "I have said these things to you, that in me you may have peace. In the world, you will have tribulation. But take heart; I have overcome the world."

In his eye-opening book, David Biebel, doctor of ministry, says that modern-day believers are, in a sense, disillusioned because we look at suffering to be something like "when the extra Mercedes is broken down or when the dishwasher is broken or the grocery store has run out of kiwis." He goes on to say, "Painless suffering is a modern phenomenon, perhaps linked to the developments of modern science aimed at eradicating disease and alleviating pain. Until recently in history, people expected pain and knew how to live with suffering."[3]

So what is the problem with disillusionment? When you hit a real trial in life, you'll likely become angry and disgruntled and walk away from your faith in God, believing you've been lied to. If we have allowed ourselves to become disillusioned, our focus is on self-gratification and not on the purposes God has for us. His purpose is for us to shine for His glory regardless of our circumstances. The phrase "light is most beneficial in darkness" is very applicable here.

James Merritt hits the point straight on in *God, I've Got a Question*: "Yet without God, there can be neither any purpose behind evil or suffering nor any final resolution to it. Only God, who can use suffering for a greater purpose, can bring meaning to it. Only a God who can use evil for His glory and the ultimate good of others can give assurance that justice will prevail."[4]

I would say it's not only God who can bring meaning to suffering, but we can too. I'd venture to say this is not only something God can do, but as we are called to be like Him, we too can use our suffering to bring about good. Anything that we have suffered can be turned around and used for good.

Walking through trials has a way of pulling back the blinders and melting away the disillusionment. I started to see God, His character,

3. Biebel, *If God Is So Good*, 79–80.
4. James Merrit, *God, I've Got a Question* (Eugene, OR: Harvest House Publishers, 2011), 87.

and His sovereignty more clearly. I started to embrace the fact that God looks at the *larger story.* He has a better perspective. He has an eternal perspective. I, on the other hand, have a "right now" perspective. I have a "this hurts" perspective. I have a "What about me?" perspective.

David B. Biebel has written that it is spiritually immature to view healing as a kind of reward for the strength or perfection of one's faith. He explained that such thinking shifts the focus away from God's sovereignty and places it instead on human effort, as though God could be manipulated by our ability to believe hard enough. His perspective put words to the very tension I have felt—that faith was never meant to be a performance test, but a trust in the God who heals according to His wisdom and will.

PEOPLE MAY TRY TO ANSWER YOUR *WHY* FOR YOU

Often, people assume that if we have major trials in our lives, then there must be a reason for it. When you are in a trial, people, even well-meaning friends or complete strangers, often try to answer your *why* for you. Joni Eareckson Tada, the founder of a worldwide ministry called Joni & Friends, had others, even strangers, trying to answer her *why.* When Joni was seventeen years old, she dove headfirst into the water and broke her neck. She became a quadriplegic from this accident and was not able to do anything for herself afterward except talk. All they could do with her all day long was to flip her from one side to the other. She could stare at the ceiling, or she could stare at the floor. She couldn't even scratch her nose if she wanted to. You'd think someone in this condition would never hope to accomplish anything again, although she finally gained the ability to be wheelchair-bound.

One day, Joni had a young man named David come up to her after church. He announced he was a visitor, and he asked if he could pray for her healing. She replied, "Well, I never refuse prayer!" The man launched into what, Joni said, sounded like a prepared speech. "Well, Joni, have you ever considered that it may be sin standing in the way of your healing?" He flipped open his Bible to the book of Luke and read, "Some men came carrying a paralyzed man on a sleeping mat. They tried to take him inside to Jesus, but they couldn't reach him because of the crowd. So they went up to the roof and took off some tiles. Then they lowered the sick man on his mat down into the crowd, right in front of Jesus" (5:18–19). David exclaimed to Joni that the paralyzed man in the story had been healed, and that she could be too if she would only confess her sins and have faith to believe.

"Joni, there must be something in your life that you haven't dealt with yet." She told him that her conscience was clean before the Lord. He looked a little skeptical. She thanked him for his concern, then she told him she didn't think this was a matter of faith. For David, that just didn't add up. According to what he had been taught, if Joni was a Christian and there was no known sin in her life, the faith she had in God "should" heal her. She should be healed. He persisted, "Joni, you must have a lack of faith. I mean, look at you. You're still in your wheelchair!" Joni thought for a moment about the biblical account he had just read, then she asked him to open his Bible again to that same passage. Then Joni said to him,

> "Okay, you're right about one thing, David. Right after they lowered the paralyzed man through the roof onto the floor in front of Jesus, he was healed. But look at verse 20. It says that when Jesus saw the faith of those four friends, the man was made well. So? Don't you see? He didn't require anything at all from the disabled man; what he was looking for was faith in those men who lowered him through the roof. God doesn't require *my* faith for healing. But he may require *yours.* The pressure's off me, David. If God has it in his plan to lift me out of this wheelchair, he could use *your* faith! So, keep believing, friend, the pressure is on *you!*"[5]

Joni met all the requirements David proposed, but she still wasn't healed. Why? Joni used this event in her life to show that suffering, at times, is simply a part of the Christian life. You see, after much anger and wrestling with God, Joni found emotional and spiritual healing and wholeness, and she was able to go on to learn how to draw amazing

---

5. Joni Eareckson Tada, *A Place of Healing* (Colorado: Dave Cook, 2010), 16–17.

pictures using an art utensil in her mouth. She not only became a famous artist, but she also became a successful and influential Christian author, speaker, singer, counselor, and advocate for disabled people. If any of us accomplished just one of those things in our lifetime, we'd feel satisfied. I'd venture to say she has done these things not *despite* her disability, but quite likely even *because* of this all-consuming thorn in her flesh.

God often uses hardship to use us in the world and to prepare us for eternity. This process is called sanctification. Sometimes it includes trials, loss, and an overwhelming amount of pain. Most people recognize that struggle builds character and perseverance, yet we avoid it at all costs. We resist it, deny it, and often see it as a problem to be solved.

Joni found healing and joy in life again, not in the way she would have desired, but in a way that allowed God to use her more powerfully than ever before. Her healing wasn't physical; it was spiritual. God allowed her trial because it shaped her, sanctified her, and gave her a testimony that continues to bless the world.

In the end, Joni found real faith in God. She found much more than things she could do well; she found a reason for being, a purpose in her life, no matter what limitations she faced. She found her *why*.

WHAT IS THE ULTIMATE ANSWER?

Ultimately, we turn to God because He is the only Source for any real answer. His knowledge has no limits. He is all-powerful, all-knowing, and ever-present. He alone holds an eternal plan that offers hope. He alone has shown us such sacrificial love.

As author Randy Alcorn puts it, "We must not simply believe in God, but believe *what is true about God*."[6] It's so easy to shape God into who we want Him to be, but that isn't faith in God, that is faith in our expectations. People likely don't walk away from God because they

---

6. Randy Alcorn, *If God Is Good: Faith in the Midst of Suffering and Evil* (Colorado: Multnomah Books, 2009), 36.

found out He isn't who He says He is; they walk away because they found out He doesn't fit into their box.

The truth is that God is sovereign, meaning He possesses the power, wisdom, and authority to do anything, but that doesn't mean He is in complete control of everything that happens. That doesn't mean He causes everything that happens. Although we may hate that suffering has some part in the plan, we must face its reality in our lives and balance that out with the truth of God's love.

Here is what we know to be true of God:

- God loves us deeply.
- He is trustworthy.
- He is sovereign and wise, yet considers our opinion as a good father would.
- He works all things for our good.
- He has an eternal plan for our lives.
- And He gave the ultimate sacrifice just to be in relationship with us.

When we truly see and understand not only God's character but the depth of God's love for us, we can believe His choices are good even if we don't understand His reasons. Isaiah 55:8–9 (ESV) says, "For my thoughts are not your thoughts, neither are your ways my ways, declares the LORD. For as the heavens are higher than the earth, so are my ways higher than your ways and my thoughts than your thoughts."

LAYING DOWN OUR QUESTIONS & PICKING UP OUR CROSS

We struggle with pain and suffering, and it should be no wonder. We must remember that Jesus's disciples and Jesus Himself struggled with the cross and what Jesus foretold about His death. We have a hard time trusting what we don't understand. So, when we reach a point with God that we can't understand, we may question, grow disillusioned, or even consider walking away. But God hasn't called us to trust in *ourselves, our plans,* or *our wisdom*—He's called us to a life of faith in Him, His plan, and His wisdom.

Some of the best and most succinct answers I found in my search for *why* we must endure pain and suffering came in these words aimed at counseling teens: "Avoid simplistic or overly spiritualized answers. Yes, Jesus saves, but often, He leads us through a long path of insight and growth so that we learn valuable lessons from the suffering we endure. Most of the time, He rescues us through our pain, not out of our pain."[7] That is the hard truth we need to face. Often, God rescues us *through* our pain, not *out of* our pain!

THE QUESTION YOU MUST ANSWER

I finally figured out that it all boiled down to one question. And that question wasn't for God, it was for me. Was I willing to trust God even if I didn't have the answers or if the answers I received weren't what I was hoping for? Perhaps that question is for you, as well. Friend, are you willing to trust God even if you don't receive the answers or if the answers you receive aren't what you are hoping for? Can you trust what you do know of God more than what you don't understand about Him?

Even Job had to come to this conclusion. Even after all his suffering and questioning, he finally concluded that knowing God was better than knowing answers (see Job 42:5–6). We must turn from our desire for logic or understanding of our circumstances and turn to faith and trust in His higher power. We must put our full trust in Him.

God wants us to come to the end of ourselves, because only when we do that will we start to see Him. We get our focus back. We must learn to lay down our *why* and pick up our cross.

Dear Lord,

I believe in Your wisdom, power, and love above all things. Lord, I will trust You even with those prayers that have not been answered. I will trust You even with the plans I don't like. I will trust You. Strengthen me, Lord, never to give up, never to lose faith, and to endure through every circumstance. I will walk by

---

7. Tim Clinton, Chap Clark, and Joshua Straub, *The Quick-Reference Guide to Counseling Teenagers* (Grand Rapids, MI: Baker Books, 2010), 276.

faith, not by sight. Lord, I hold onto Your promise of the crown of life (James 1:12); my hope is in You.

In Jesus's mighty name, amen.

PART TWO

NAVIGATING THE FLOOD OF FEELINGS

CHAPTER 4

PROCESSING YOUR
GRIEF EMOTIONS

Those who plant in tears
will harvest with shouts of joy.
They weep as they go to plant their seed,
but they sing as they return with the harvest.
—Psalm 126:5–6

Sometimes, people avoid grief, put it off, or shove it aside, perhaps because it feels too overwhelming, or they may not know how to express it. Or, as a Christian, they may even feel it's wrong to express their grief. But grief doesn't just go away; it's like having a heavy backpack full of rocks that gets strapped on our backs. We don't get to choose whether we carry the grief; it's placed on our shoulders, often without warning. At first, we might try to ignore it, thinking that if we just move forward, it will go away on its own. But no matter how hard we try, the weight is still there—it doesn't just disappear. We can try to pretend it's not heavy, shift it around, or even ignore the pain, but eventually, it will catch up with us. The only way to make it lighter isn't to shove it down or pretend it's not there. It's to take the time to open the backpack and take out the rocks, one by one, and chip away at them. Some rocks are heavier than others, and some take longer to chip away at or put down, but each time you process a piece of grief, the load gets a little lighter.

My perception of grief, before the loss of my son, was that it was just a great sadness you had to get through. Now I know that grief is a myriad of intense emotions potentially including sadness, anger, guilt, fear, confusion, worry, jealousy, annoyance, anxiety, bitterness, blame, compassion, concern, feeling dazed, denial, devastation, relief, abandonment, vulnerability, rage, shock, heartbreak, and irritability, that is a lot of rocks you may be carrying around. Our GriefShare workbook shared over 160 different common responses and emotions that may be experienced after the death of a loved one.[1] And unfortunately, you will have these emotions coming and going, intruding at the least expected moments; they will leave you feeling lost, numb, and confused. It is normal to have this ball of emotions bombarding your heart and mind at this time. A lot of the bewildering things you're going through are a natural response to your loss.

WHY GRIEF EMOTIONS NEED EXPRESSION

Emotions are the natural state of mind we are in because of our circumstances, moods, or relationships with others. With grief, the emotions are so numerous and confusing that it's hard to function normally because we can't see past those emotions. What do we do with all these emotions? Normally, when we are *not* experiencing a trauma, we handle the emotions we deal with on a day-to-day basis. They are far fewer, less intense, and less fluctuating. But when we are going through grief, the sheer number of emotions we go through, the depth of their intensity, and the fact that they are in constant *replay* can be utterly overwhelming.

You must confront your grief, loss, and trauma associated with death by suicide. Experts say if you attempt to ignore it—sweep it under the carpet of your life—you may only be delaying an even deeper pain. Some people have suffered breakdowns *decades* after a suicide

---

1. GriefShare, *Your Journey from Mourning to Joy*, 4–5.

because they refused or were forbidden to ever talk about it."[2] Friend, it's essential to work through your grief. Don't tuck it away, or at the other extreme, get lost in it.

Why Suppressing Emotions is Bad for Your Health

Research shows that repressing or suppressing your emotions is bad for your mental and physical health. However, releasing or processing emotions can enhance your physical and mental health. According to psychotherapist Emily Roberts,

> Research suggests that suppressing emotions is associated with high rates of heart disease, as well as autoimmune disorders, ulcers, IBS, and gastrointestinal health complications. Whether you are experiencing anger, sadness, grief, or frustration, pushing those feelings aside actually leads to physical stress on your body. Studies show that holding in feelings correlates with high cortisol—the hormone released in response to stress—and that cortisol leads to lower immunity and toxic thinking patterns. Over time, untreated or unrecognized stress can lead to an increased risk of diabetes, problems with memory, aggression, anxiety, and depression.[3]

Simply put, we *must* process our emotions, and the need is all the greater during traumatic grief.

Feelings Must Come Up and Out—Like Vomit

In counseling, I learned that to be healed, those emotions must come up and out. I even had one counselor tell me, "It's like vomit when you're sick." When we are physically sick, our body knows it needs to expel whatever ailment is causing our sickness. But oftentimes, when we are emotionally sick, we tend not to release that pain. We often

---

2. Jackson, *A Handbook for Coping with Suicide Grief*, 3.
3. Emily Roberts, "Why You Need to Release Your Emotions—For the Sake of Your Health," *Mbg Health,* November 18, 2018, https://www.mindbodygreen.com/articles/suppressing-your-emotions-physical-health.

stuff pain. Hide pain. Ignore pain. Imagine swallowing and stuffing down your vomit, hoping you can just move on, and the sickness will somehow disappear. Yet, if we never do anything to work through and process our pain so it can be safely released, it can destroy us from the inside out. If not released, these emotions can produce a poisonous brew of anger, bitterness, and hopelessness inside of us. Yet, Psalm 62:8 directs us to "trust in him at all times. Pour out your heart to him, for God is our refuge." This shows that God is looking for us to pour out our emotions; He is there for us.

Further, this processing of emotions is not a one-time event. Today may be just rounds one through seven of a potentially one-thousand-round bout. Some of the emotions I commonly fought in these bouts were fear, anger, confusion, and guilt. There is something about confessing things and bringing them out in the open that cleanses us of them. It's not that they will be immediately gone—because they likely won't—but you feel the difference between hiding and storing them versus confessing and revealing.

We must cry it out. Think it out. Scream it out. It's a natural part of grief. We are always taught to run from pain, but there is no running from this pain; eventually, we must face it. Repressing our emotions, especially in suicide grief, is common, in part because of the stigma, whether real or perceived, around suicide. We must be extra-diligent in suicide grief to express, not repress, those emotions and realize we have every right to do so. We need to acknowledge how we are feeling and realize that it's okay to feel.

Below, I've listed some things that seemed to help me get my feelings up and out. I used every one of these avenues, but my main vehicle of choice was journaling (of course). Perhaps this list will help you as well.

- speaking with others
- praying to God
- speaking with a counselor
- joining a grief share group (of any type) and *participating*
- writing things out (One way to do this is to consider each consuming emotion: fear, anger, guilt, etc. Write the

emotion at the top of a blank page, then get those feelings of anger out on the page. Why are you angry? Who are you angry at? And so on.)

- going somewhere privately and speaking about how you're feeling aloud to yourself
- creating art that brings up those emotions, for example, poems, drawings, paintings, etc.
- screaming them out (when you're all alone)
- physically smashing them out—for example, find a dead tree to demolish with a fallen limb, whatever you can do that is safe for you and others
- breathing exercises and stretching or relaxation routines (I used these a lot. I almost *had to* do them in order to quell the anxiety so I could go to sleep at night.)

Don't torture yourself. Maybe you even think, *I deserve this pain! I deserve this hurt. I won't release it because I deserve it.* I felt this way, too, but slowly, I realized my life isn't all about me. I have others who depend on me. And just because I had to suffer a horrible, tragic pain doesn't mean the rest of my life can't hold beauty, even while I work at expelling the beast of pain.

Who Will Rule Your Emotions?

God created our emotions, but it is who we allow to rule over those emotions that will determine who gets the glory for them or how we perceive them. Romans 8:6 reads, "So letting your sinful nature control your mind leads to death. But letting the Spirit control your mind leads to life and peace." God's intent for the emotion of guilt was meant to lead us to repentance, but Satan misuses guilt to try to destroy us, to bring us low. God uses pain to warn us of danger, but Satan uses pain to torture us. God uses our emotions of hate and anger so we know what it is to hate sin, but Satan uses hate to get us to fight against each other. God may use sadness so we will be sad over our sin, but Satan uses sadness to condemn us for our sin. God uses impatience to help us to strive for things; Satan uses impatience to exasperate us.

For every single emotion God has given us, Satan has a counterfeit that leads to destruction. God has a plan to use it for good, but Satan steps in, trying to confuse us. We must recognize the intentions behind each emotion and understand how they can be used for our benefit or exploited against us for our destruction. Satan works to wear us down[4] while the Lord works to build us up.[5]

Let's look at a few Scriptures. First Peter 5:8 warns us, "Stay alert! Watch out for your great enemy, the devil. He prowls around like a roaring lion, looking for someone to devour." Yet in the same way, 2 Chronicles 16:9 encourages us, "The eyes of the LORD search the whole earth in order to strengthen those whose hearts are fully committed to him." You see, the Lord and Satan are both chasing after us. Who will you allow to rule in your life?

EMOTIONALLY CRIPPLED, ARE YOU STUCK IN GRIEF?

If we don't work at processing our emotions, or we allow Satan to rule over our emotions, we can become stuck in grief, or what I would call emotionally crippled. This has no benefit, and it would only serve to hurt us and the rest of our family. After a loss, anyone who allows themselves to become stuck in grief is walking right into Satan's trap. I knew he had already worked illness in my son's life to take him away. I was not about to give Satan one more inch by allowing myself or my family to become stuck in grief that would eventually destroy us, as well. Therefore, I became proactive for all of us to learn about the issues surrounding our loss so that we could properly heal.

What does it mean to be stuck in grief? In my GriefShare program, we learned that being stuck in grief is when you stay in the same place, and you don't make an effort to move forward through grief as you should. If you don't take steps to leave this place, you can put your life at a standstill, and some people who get "stuck" in grief never seem to be able to move forward in life. Camping out in the "valley of the shadow of death" cannot be healthy. Therefore, it is important to

---

4. Danel 7:25 ESV
5. Isaiah 41:10 ESV

process our grieving emotions so we can heal and move forward out of the valley. I finally came to realize through counseling, prayer, and study that my purpose for living didn't cease with my son's death. The rest of my family members needed me. And God still had work for me to do.

My GriefShare leader told me people typically get stuck by staying on things they cannot change. She said, "This is Satan's grand arsenal. Don't fall for it! Recognize Satan is attempting to destroy you." She would often say, "We need to accept the things we cannot change." What are the things you may get stuck on? Believing it was your fault? Angrily believing the loss of your loved one was someone else's fault? Believing you can't move on because it wouldn't show the depth of love you still have for your lost loved one? We need to be aware of becoming emotionally crippled. This means we need to be cautious of getting stuck on those things we cannot change. Choosing to leave or rid ourselves of bad, wrong, or lying feelings is something only we can do. Choosing to walk through our grief is something only we can do. Others can help and guide us, but we must choose to do the hard work of grieving and processing our emotions.

DON'T LET FALSE BELIEFS DISTORT YOUR EMOTIONS

When I felt that barrier or distance between God and myself that I talked about in a previous chapter, I felt like I couldn't trust Him. I felt like I didn't love Him anymore because He had "allowed" this to happen. It seemed my relationship with God was being dismantled. I knew the truth, but I couldn't feel the truth. I remembered what His Word promised, but I couldn't feel it. I knew the love I had experienced when He had shown up in my life so many times before, but I couldn't sense that love in my deep grief. Jeremiah 17:9 says it this way: "The human heart is the most deceitful of all things, and desperately wicked." This is a good indication that we can't always trust our feelings. It's not that what you are feeling is a lie. If you feel an emotion (fear, anger, bitterness, guilt, etc.), you truly feel that way. But your heart beliefs produce those emotions, and your beliefs can be based on misinformation or things that simply aren't true. If we then use those distorted feelings to inform our thoughts and actions, things can get pretty messy. Why? "Fools think their own way is right, but the wise listen to others" (Proverbs 12:15). We reason with ourselves and think, *If I feel "this way," it must be true. It must be right.* But God knows us better than we know ourselves. I slowly began to realize that my feelings didn't match up to the reality of my previous experiences with God. I knew my feelings were being overridden with my current circumstance of grief. So, my feelings were falling prey to my circumstances.

If we share how we are feeling with God, He can redirect our beliefs to the truth. But we must seek Him. We must allow the Holy Spirit to lead us into all truth (see John 16:13). He will truly direct our paths if we seek Him. We must spend time with God, pray, look for answers in His Word, and be open to Him speaking to us. It's only natural that as we learn more about God and His character, we come to understand His love for us. And as we see that love He has for us, we will naturally be inspired to trust our lives to Him regardless of our circumstances.

CALL OUT TO GOD

Have you ever wondered why God wants us to share with Him in prayer if He already knows everything? God tells us in 1 Peter 5:7, "Give all your worries and cares to God, for he cares about you." God knows our future. He already knows our past. He knows our present. But have you ever considered that God may just want us to pray because it is good for us? It releases our worries, our anxieties, our pain, and our bitterness. God knows it is a way of purging, purifying, cleansing, releasing, relieving, freeing, delivering, ridding, and exorcizing our pain, bitterness, and confusion.

John Eldridge has two great books, *Get Your Life Back* and *Resilient,* that help us acquire emotional resilience through Christ. John Eldridge also has a free app called the Pause app, which is based on his books about emotional resilience. It doesn't speak specifically to suicide grief, rather it fosters mental and emotional resilience through Christ and includes such applications as meditations, journaling, prayer, etc. I found these resources especially helpful during grief, when it can be difficult to connect with God. They provide great guidance for your quiet time. The engaging app acts as a guide, helping you draw near to God and give Him *everyone* and *everything* that weighs on your heart. Share your pain with God. He can bring comfort to you even in grief.

Why Finding Safe People Is Important

One of my suggested avenues for getting our emotions up and out is through using someone else as a sounding board. My GriefShare counselor stressed the importance of making sure to "find safe people" when you do this. People often stuff emotions inside themselves because they feel like it's the only safe place for them to be "allowed." One thing I heard in my GriefShare program was, "Fear Hates Community." I love the truth of that statement. There is healing in simply getting the feelings up and out, but we must remember that we need to find safe people to do this with. As my counselor reminded us time after time, "There are safe people we can allow to participate in our pain, and there are others that will, likely unintentionally, hurt us more." Find your safe people.

Emotional Strongholds and How to Tear Them Down

Emotional strongholds occur when we judge our feelings and circumstances according to false beliefs, rebellious thoughts, and the lies Satan spins, and *not* according to God's Word and what He says about us. These emotional strongholds can control us and, ultimately, our actions. If our emotions stem from lies, we must replace those lies with the truth of God's Word.

Take guilt, for example. I wanted to blame myself in so many ways for my son's death, but as I talked through these emotions with my GriefShare leader, she helped me to see that these thoughts were lies because they weren't based on the truth. What I believed wasn't true; it was only arguments or self-deception. These thought patterns I was caught in were strongholds Satan was erecting to destroy me; I sure didn't want to help him build on them, so I had to see them for what they were. Just like Satan deceived Eve, he can easily do the same with us.

I asked my GriefShare leader why, even though I kept praying for a particular emotion to leave me, it kept returning. And why was it so hard for me to see the truth of the situation? She reminded me, "A lot of times when we pray about something, and nothing seems to happen, we wonder if God is hearing us, but it may not be that God isn't hearing us, but more likely that what we are praying against is a stronghold. Stronghold. Strongholds are not easily removed, and therefore these prayers are not just wasted prayers, but they are tearing down strongholds blow by blow and bit by bit." People can allow strongholds to be erected in their lives at any point, but we may be even more susceptible to this during grief because we are so exhausted and fixated on our loss.

My GriefShare leader said, "Pray all your anxious thoughts through." How long? "Until your heart and mind are guarded through Christ Jesus." So often, we'll pray on something and think we're done. We gave it to God. However, we often pick it back up again. And that means we need to pray, giving it back to God every time it resurfaces. We need to replace that lie with the truth of God's Word. It is a continual battle in grief, but for our hearts and minds to be guarded by Christ Jesus, we must continue until it sticks—until we have complete victory over it. Only then will your heart and mind be guarded from these invading, destructive thoughts. My GriefShare leader said, "If we do any less (than giving it all to God), it's only positive thinking." When we give Christ complete control, then and only then will we rest our minds from it.

The Scripture she used to help us with this point is Philippians 4:5–7 (ESV), which says, "The Lord is at hand; do not be anxious about anything, but in everything by prayer and supplication with thanksgiving let your requests be made known to God. And the peace of God, which surpasses all understanding, will guard your hearts and your minds in Christ Jesus." When we give it all to God, we are focusing on God for our deliverance, not on overcoming this situation in ourselves. When we give these strongholds to God consistently, He sees we are trusting and believing on Him for deliverance and super-natural peace.

When battling these false feelings and emotions, it's important to find specific Scriptures to stand on—to meditate on. If you are battling lies, hand them over to God, no matter how many times you must do it. If we don't tear down these strongholds, they can have us believing things about God that aren't true. I had to work through a lot of things with God to help me see that some of my feelings were misdirecting my actions toward God, discrediting God, and creating bitterness, anger, and a sense of abandonment.

So, every prayer we pray is slowly but surely weakening that strong-hold. Every time we refuse to pick these things back up again, that evil stronghold is taking another blow. Every time we replace those lies with a truth found in God's Word, we are building a new stronghold—a stronghold of faith. God wants us to make Him the stronghold of our lives, as Psalm 9:9 (NASB 1995) tells us: "The LORD also will be a strong-hold for the oppressed, A stronghold in times of trouble." We are to have a stronghold in our lives, but it's not the negative strongholds that often come to mind. Psalm 27:1 (ESV) tells us what that stronghold should be: "The LORD is my light and my salvation; whom shall I fear? The LORD is the stronghold of my life; of whom shall I be afraid?" Friends, we must make the Lord the stronghold of our lives.

So how do we operate with God as our stronghold, and how do we wage war against these evil strongholds? God's Word says, "We are human, but we don't wage war as humans do. We use God's mighty weapons, not worldly weapons, to knock down the strongholds of human reasoning and to destroy false arguments. We destroy every proud obstacle that keeps people from knowing God. We capture these rebellious thoughts and teach them to obey Christ" (2 Corinthians 10:3–5).

The Scripture above shows us that strongholds are arguments, lofty opinions, and thoughts raised against the knowledge of God. These wrong emotions, thoughts, or beliefs can become so strong that they can lead to other damaging emotions or actions, potentially even walking away from God. Further, this Scripture lets us know we are to use God's weapons, not worldly weapons. So, what are God's weapons? His Word, the Holy Spirit, fasting, prayer, truth, love, etc. What are the world's weapons? Human reasoning, false arguments, or anything we try to do in our own power. As followers of Christ, we don't wage war in the same way other humans do. We tap into God's weapons and wield them because only through them do we find supernatural power, understanding, truth, and freedom—freedom from emotional strongholds.

For example, when feelings of anger or blame arise, or when I ask myself *why* questions, I ask God to take them from me. I ask Him to give me calm, grace, or peace in this area. In the same way that the evil strongholds are so inundating and repetitive, sometimes we must repeat and inundate our lives with the good stronghold by repeating and memorizing Scripture for the battle.

I prayed daily for healing from my grief, not just for myself but for my whole family. I found Scripture to battle those specific areas of weakness. Slowly, these hurtful emotions will be replaced with what God wants in us. If we continue to hand it over to God and rely on Him and His Word, eventually that bitterness, anger, guilt, self-hate, confusion, or the myriad of other hurtful emotions are either completely disintegrated or they become so weak that when they do come back, we will have no problem telling them off as the lies they are.

I hope you can see how important it is to process our grief emotions. Don't hide them, stuff them, or pretend they don't exist. Satan wants to misuse your emotions against you. Don't let him have any more victories. Today, take a moment to write down how you are feeling. As you are able, take each of those emotions and look at them. Write out whether they stem from the truth or lies. Write out God's Word that refutes lies, wrong thoughts, or beliefs. Recognize the things you cannot change and begin to accept them. It may be good even to write out those things you cannot change with a bold title that reads *THINGS I CANNOT CHANGE*. Hand all that you find over to God. Do this until your heart and mind are guarded in Christ Jesus.

Dear Lord,

I have planted in tears; help me to harvest healing. Lord, I give You access to my heart. You see this ball of emotions I'm full of. Help me to truthfully look at each emotion, process it, and lay it at Your feet. You knew we would need a listening ear. Thank You for being that for me. You knew if we kept our bad emotions in, they could make us sick. Thank You that I can talk to You anytime and anywhere about any and every emotion I'm feeling. Even when I feel like You have messed up my life, help me to see the truth. Give me wisdom to battle the emotional strongholds that Satan is attempting to erect in my life. Lord, help me to find peace in You.

In Jesus's name, amen.

CHAPTER 5

LAYING DOWN YOUR GUILT

My guilt overwhelms me—it is a burden too heavy to bear.
—Psalm 38:4

I'm sure you're not surprised that guilt got its own chapter. It's pure hell. In losing my child to suicide, there were three overpowering emotions: sadness, fear, and guilt. Guilt was the one that worked a twenty-four-hour shift, woke me in the middle of the night, and plagued me all day long.

Guilt was the largest emotional boulder that blocked my path to life, and it seemed no matter how much I chipped away at it, it loomed largest. In suicide grief, guilt is likely a big boulder for us all. Jamie Winship masterfully defines guilt as "belief that our sin has the final word,"[1] and that definition captured what I didn't even know I believed. But as you'll see in this chapter, guilt does *not* have the final word. God does.

---

1. Jamie Winship, *Living Fearless Guided Journal* (Redding, CA: Igniting Souls Publishing Agency, 2021), 92.

YOU CAN'T DO BETTER THAN NOT KNOWING

As previously mentioned, Satan tries to misuse the emotions God has given us, and one of those emotions is guilt. God uses guilt to convict us of sin, but Satan uses guilt to trap and destroy us from the inside.

My GriefShare leader asked me what I was blaming myself for. There were many things; I should have gone on the trip my son and his dad took. Maybe my son would have talked to me then. I should not have gone back to school; I was too busy when he came over a few times. I should have researched depression more. I should have pushed for medication more. I should have done more. Realized more. Thought more. Prayed more. I should have *been more*. I should have known what I didn't know. I should have been a better mom. But I wasn't, and now my son was gone. I didn't know my son was sick to this extent.

Maria, my GriefShare leader, gave me some words that seemed to help somewhat: "You can't do better than not knowing. You would never have wanted this to happen." She was right. If I didn't know my son was at this point of no return, I had to admit, I didn't know. She also helped by reminding me to see, "You did the best you could at the time mentally, physically, and spiritually." Although we knew we weren't perfect parents, we did know that we gave parenting our all. How can you give more than your all?

Friend, can you see this in your situation? Let me say it for you. Whether you are a parent, sibling, spouse, friend, or loved one, you would have never wanted this to happen. You likely didn't know, and you can't do better than not knowing. And even if you did know of your loved one's struggles, it doesn't mean you understood the depth or the potential outcome. Furthermore, I'm sure you did the best you could mentally, physically, and spiritually. Take peace in that.

HOW TO DECIPHER FALSE GUILT AND ELIMINATE IT

We have false guilt when we feel guilty, but we have not truly sinned or done wrong. It is false guilt when what we are blaming ourselves for simply isn't true. In one of the first meetings I had with my GriefShare leader, she had me write down on paper everything I was blaming myself for. Then, on another page, she had me draw a heading with a dividing line down the center. In the section headings, she had me write "True Guilt versus False Guilt." She said, "Now look at each area you are blaming yourself for, then ask, 'Is this really true? Was I really to blame for my loved one's death? Is this what I would have wanted to happen?'" Looking at true and false guilt can seem irrelevant to us because we think if we *feel* guilty, then we must *be* guilty. If you are having this issue, it may help to have a counselor or pastor help you to decipher the difference between what is true guilt and what is false guilt.

Satan tries to convince us to hang onto the guilt; God tries to remind us He has already established a plan for our forgiveness, in every way. Romans 8:1 reads, "So now there is no condemnation for those who belong to Christ Jesus." I memorized this Scripture, and every time guilt attacked, I'd throw it out by quoting this verse. You can, too.

Often, we feel like hanging onto guilt as a way to punish ourselves. If we do this, we may not fully understand God's pardon. When we try to blame ourselves for something God does not blame us for, we are putting ourselves above Him. In essence, we are saying we know better than God does. Jesus bought our freedom, yet we refuse to allow ourselves that freedom.

My counselor was also quick to remind me of 2 Corinthians 10:4–5 (NIV), which says, "The weapons we fight with are not the weapons of the world. On the contrary, they have divine power to demolish strongholds. We demolish arguments and every pretension that sets itself up

against the knowledge of God, and we take captive every thought to make it obedient to Christ."

When we lie to ourselves, believing this false guilt, we are setting ourselves up against the knowledge of God. God tells us to take every thought captive. After we capture the thought, then we must look at it and decide whether it is true or not. Anything that is not true is against God. Therefore, we are going against God when we believe the lies that we or the enemy tries to perpetuate in our lives. These lies not

only keep us from healing in our grief, but also keep us from a relationship with God.

Maria, my GriefShare leader, would say, "Christ forgave you; are
you greater than Him? He wants to set you free; punishing yourself
only prevents your healing. It's not God's plan for you to beat yourself
up. And it certainly doesn't honor your son." Speak these words over
yourself: "Christ forgave me; am I greater than Him? He wants to set
me free; punishing myself only prevents my healing. It's not God's plan
for me to beat myself up. And it certainly doesn't honor my lost loved
one."

WHAT DO WE DO WITH TRUE GUILT?

We must examine any areas of true guilt and determine if there is
anything we can improve in our lives for ourselves and our loved ones.
I've had to face the fact that we may not have done everything
completely right by Haden. Were we good parents for the most part?
Yes. But might we have missed something because we were too
consumed with our own lives? Too busy? Yes. Can we do anything
about that now for Haden? No, but we can make him proud of how we
live from now on. We can be honest with ourselves, even if it hurts,
and see that we are addressing any other issues with each other and our
other children if there are problems.

If you must face areas of true guilt that encompass ways you could
have done better, then by all means, make positive change in those
areas.

WHAT TO DO WITH NEGATIVE EMOTIONS ABOUT SUICIDE

The way we interpret our loved one's suicide deeply affects our ability
to process our grief, extend forgiveness (to ourselves, others, or even
our loved one), and ultimately find healing. If we view suicide solely
through the lens of shame, criminality, or selfishness, we may be seeing
it through layers of fear, confusion, stigma, and misinformation.
Suppose we recognize it as a desperate act often influenced by mental
illness, unbearable psychological pain, or distorted thinking. In that

case, we may find it easier to approach our grief with compassion and understanding. (We'll explore this further in chapter 8: "Suicide Stigma: Building a Bridge to Understanding.")

I believe my son's death was not the result of hatred or weakness. It was not malice, not a simple matter of choice, and not an act of self-ishness—but the outcome of deep psychological pain that clouded his ability to see another way forward.

Negative emotions come with all types of grief, but with suicide grief, these emotions can envelop you and send you trudging through a personal hell you may never leave if you don't fight for your healing. I was not above feelings of betrayal, bitterness, rage, abandonment, and heartbreak with suicide loss. I had to wrestle with these emotions repeatedly. One truth that helped me was reminding myself that my son was suffering. And my guess is his pain was greater than any experience I'd had except maybe my suffering his loss.

In my research, I came across a book filled with tragic stories of suicide loss. It recounted the pain of grieving families, but it did so in a way that seemed to dwell on anger and bitterness rather than offering a path toward healing. Some of the individuals shared how they harbored deep resentment toward their loved ones, believing their deaths to be intentional betrayals. I didn't finish the book because my goal was not just to grieve but to find hope, healing, and recovery—not only for myself and my family but also as a way to honor Haden's life.

It was heartbreaking to see how some suicide grievers may have remained trapped in judgment toward their loved ones, unable to see past their pain. If this is where you find yourself, please know that these feelings are valid, but they also signal a need for support, care, and a deeper understanding of suicide. Grief can cloud our perspectives, and sometimes, without meaning to, we hold onto beliefs that may not fully reflect the complexity of our loved one's suffering.

Some survivors continue believing that their loved ones deliberately chose to leave them, concluding that if they genuinely cared, they wouldn't have died this way. But grief and the pain that entails can distort reality. Just as we would never accuse a cancer patient of taking "the easy way out," or blame an Alzheimer's patient for their illness, or condemn a loved one for dying of heart disease, we must be careful with the way we frame suicide. Pain is complex. Mental distress can alter a person's ability to see hope. And while we may not fully understand our loved one's internal battle, we can acknowledge that their struggle was real. Instead of holding onto anger or resentment, we can recognize their pain, understand that they weren't trying to hurt us, and realize that their actions came from suffering, not a lack of love.

Sadly, many grieving families also carry anger over the way others judge suicide loss. They may feel the weight of stigma and stereotypes, yet without realizing it, they sometimes place the same labels on their deceased loved ones.

This is not the road to healing. Bitterness keeps us trapped in pain. If we want to move toward wholeness, forgiveness is essential—not just for our loved one, but for ourselves. And even if we struggle with how to define choice regarding suicide, acknowledging the depth of suffering that leads to such a place can be an important step toward healing.

This doesn't mean we excuse what happened or even pretend it didn't hurt us. It may just mean the difference between saying, "How could you do this to me?" and instead saying, "I wish you could have seen another way out, but I know you were hurting."

How to Forgive in the Wake of Suicide

Guilt in suicide loss is often rooted in a lack of self-forgiveness. Yet we usually must forgive more than just ourselves. We must forgive anyone we hold guilty for the loss of our loved one, whether that is God, a doctor, family members, friends, or the lost loved one themselves.

So, finding not only how to forgive but ways to battle any unforgiveness that lingers is paramount to your healing. In his book *Aftershock*, David Cox has some great advice regarding forgiveness. He shares this sentiment: When we harbor unforgiveness, it usually turns to bitterness, and with bitterness in tow, we likely will not find recovery. If we want to truly heal, we must truly forgive. He says, "Forgiveness is not a feeling. It is a powerful transaction that does not require the offending person's cooperation to take place."[2] He lets us know that forgiveness can take place between us and God alone.

While I agree that forgiveness is a transaction, feelings don't just always "go away" with that initial transaction; rather, forgiveness may *also* include a gradual process. As my husband says, "Forgiveness is a work in progress." There is the initial transaction of declaring forgiveness for God, yourself, your lost loved one, or others, followed by a continual process of handing over any newly sprouted feelings of unforgiveness to God. Just like true repentance involves more than words—it requires a genuine change of heart and attitude—so does forgiveness. It is not something we just say; it's something we live out, often daily, as we allow our hearts to be reshaped by God and His Word.

With that said, I do believe God can also provide a miraculous ability to forgive that only includes one moment in time, and for some of us, He does. But for many of us, we must process through the feelings of unforgiveness, continually laying down our pain and bitterness.

Unforgiveness is a stronghold that can be erected in our lives by our enemy, ourselves, or even blame we perceive from others, but with God's help, we can overcome it. Following is a condensed version of Cox's five steps to forgiveness:

FIVE PRACTICAL STEPS TO FORGIVENESS

1. Write down the offense, using as much detail as possible. The process of writing is a way to transfer the hurt from your heart to the paper. This transfer helps you look at the offense more objectively and allows cleansing to occur. The more specific the description, the more complete the forgiveness.
2. Tell God out loud that you release the offender from the (real or perceived) offense, even if it is God Himself.
3. If you need to ask for forgiveness for something you've said

---

2. Cox and Arrington, *Aftershock*, 122–123.

or done, do so. (Regarding asking your lost loved one for
forgiveness, you can ask God for this forgiveness.)

4. Let go of self-condemnation; forgive yourself. God promises
    us that if we confess, God casts our sins away. Claim this
    promise and live in victory.
5. Destroy the written account as an act of closure.

I love the idea of writing the letter and then later destroying it as an
act of closure because in the loss of a loved one to suicide, we *so* need
that closure. We need to feel we have resolved or settled the situation
in our minds, hearts, and souls.

THE TRUTH WILL SET YOU FREE

God has made a way for us to be truly free in this life. In God's eyes,
false guilt has no hold on you or me. True guilt can, but only if we don't
confess it and try to rectify it. Either way, we can be free in Christ.
Romans 8:1 (NKJV) reminds us, "There is therefore now no condemnation to those who are in Christ Jesus." No condemnation means no
condemnation, regardless of whether the guilt is real or perceived.

Maria, my GriefShare leader, said that if we see the truth, it would
set us free. And the truth was we didn't understand the depth of our
son's sickness, but this did bring freedom. It was like the times when I
would keep coming back to wanting to fix it, but realizing it was done.
There was *nothing* left I could do. It was out of my hands. No matter
how badly I wanted it in my hands, it was impossible. I *had* to let it go.

As for me, I'm going to forgive myself because my son Haden
wouldn't want me to blame myself. Haden wouldn't want me to blame
my husband or anyone else in our family; neither would God. We must
allow God to heal us and not stay stuck in the self-loathing and
blaming place; otherwise, we are right where Satan wants us. We can't
be at peace if we live in guilt. I'd encourage you to forgive. Forgive
God. Forgive yourself. Forgive anyone you blame. And, of course,
forgive your lost loved one.

In 1 John 3:20, it says, "Even if we feel guilty, God is greater than
our feelings, and he knows everything." Here, John speaks about loving

one another. But in this section, he includes loving ourselves and forgiving ourselves, and he helps us realize that our hearts can misdirect us. Our conscience can condemn us *even when God does not*. John lets us know that God is greater than our hearts. This means that if our guilt and God's authority could be put on a scale, God's ultimate authority far outweighs our guilt. Take peace in that, my friend.

Dear God,

Give me grace to accept with serenity the things that cannot be changed, courage to change the things which should be changed, and the wisdom to distinguish the one from the other.

Living one day at a time, enjoying one moment at a time, accepting hardship as a pathway to peace, taking, as Jesus did, this sinful world as it is, not as I would have it, trusting that You will make all things right, if I surrender to Your will, so that I may be reasonably happy in this life, and supremely happy with You forever in the next. [3]

Lord, it is hard to forgive. Help me to see not only who I may be blaming, but also help me to have forgiveness for them. It is especially hard to forgive myself, but I know if You have forgiven me, I can forgive myself. Help me to accept that guilt does not have the final word—that You do.

In Jesus's name, amen.

---

3. "Serenity Prayer," Jesus.net, accessed May 1, 2023, https://jesus.net/articles/serenity-prayer.

Chapter 6

Transforming Your Pain

The real test of a theory or way of life, however, is not whether it can
relieve pain but what it says about the pain that it cannot relieve.
In Christianity, it has great meaning.
—William Kirk Kilpatrick

In some ways, processing pain from the perspective of faith can make it harder *before* it becomes easier. How? Those who don't believe in God only have to deal with questioning fate, but we, as believers, question a God who has always professed love for us.[1] It's a confusing mix of emotions. One book that helped me wade through this sea of confusion and pain was *If God Is So Good, Why Do I Hurt So Bad?* by David B. Biebel, doctor of ministry. Not only did Biebel help me realize I was dealing with this unique confusion due to my faith, but he shared the good news that "walking with God by faith remains the only way to transform your pain into anything other than pain."[2] It sounded hopeful, but how would I wade through it all? In this chapter, we will explore how I found a way to transform my pain as a believer

1. Biebel, *If God Is So Good*, 9.
2. Ibid., 27.

and what came from that understanding. I hope that you, too, will find a way to process and transform your pain, with God's help, into a source of power and purpose.

FIGHTING AGAINST TRUTH

"God can use your trial for good!"

Cringe! I heard those words many times after the loss of my son, and honestly, they irritated me. How could anything "good" come from the tragedy of losing my son? Good? Really? The Scripture they gleaned this idea from is Romans 8:28, "And we know that God causes everything to work together for the good of those who love God and are called according to his purpose for them."

Every time I heard this sentiment, it only made me angrier. However, one day, as I was looking through some items that my son had left hanging in his room from his teenage years, I found several pages of Scripture that he had written out by hand and pinned to his walls. It was strange, but each Scripture seemed to speak to me in this present valley of death I was walking through. One of those Scriptures was that very verse—Romans 8:28—which is about the good that God brings about in our trials. Knowing this Scripture touched my son so much that he plastered it on his wall made me slow down and look at that verse a little more closely. As I studied over it and prayed, I started to see some of its truthfulness. It was as if my son was still speaking and witnessing to me of God's goodness even while he was in Heaven. What a legacy of faith!

But the hard truth was I didn't want anything about the death of my son to be "good." It was horrible. The worst thing that will likely ever happen in my life. I wanted my son's death to only be a tragedy, a sad thing, because that was how it felt to me. It made me feel like God was saying this tragedy was *good*, but I slowly realized that was far from the truth. If God works *all* things for our good, *all* things means...even the worst tragedies of our lives. Understand that God is in no way calling this *pain* good. The truth is that God weeps with us, mourns with us, and feels our loss (see Psalm 34:18;). He isn't saying that tragedy or trial in life, of any kind, is good. Instead, God is a master at taking *anything* in our lives that Satan meant for evil and turning it around so good *can* come from it. My friend, seeing, understanding, or feeling the full meaning of this Scripture may take time.

As I started to accept my new reality, I acknowledged that Satan, the master of illness, lies, and confusion, had not only taken my son but had set out to destroy our *entire* family. And as much as I wanted to balk at the idea of something good coming through this, I started to see that I was wrong because I would be working *against* God if I didn't let Him work good from it. I realized that if God could truly bring good against Satan's plans, then I was all in.

Friend, are you working against God in the same way I was? It's so hard to acknowledge and accept that God uses the worst trials in our lives and turns them for our good. His ways are definitely different and higher than our own.

FOUR WAYS WE MAY BE WORKING AGAINST GOD TO BRING GOOD

You may find that it's so hard to see anything but the tragedy that your subconscious may be working against anything good coming out of it. To work with God in bringing about the good, we must see where we may inadvertently be working against God. Following are some of these ways:

- refusing to allow the good to be seen or acknowledged
- being comforted by a relationship with the world, not by a relationship with God
- refusing to heal any emotional trauma we developed through our tragedy
- being disobedient if He has called us to do something in connection with the good He is working out

THE GOOD WHICH WAS FOUND

I slowly found acceptance and hope for all the good that can come to fruition through our tragedy. The following are a few examples of how

God worked for good in our situation; perhaps you'll find similar "good" in your own situation.

- a deeper understanding of God
- a proof-positive of my faith
- new friendships
- a greater appreciation for life
- the hurt knowledge and heart knowledge to comfort others
- a more eternally focused mindset
- a prioritizing of my life
- greater appreciation for relationships
- others' faith being strengthened, as well
- decisions were made to follow Christ
- new strengthening and emboldening in my faith
- this book, which I pray can help others
- seeing my son as an added hope for my eternity

Don't worry if the good isn't obvious or immediate, especially at first when the pain is so blinding. But God promised it, so it should be there. Perhaps one thing we may need to do is look for it. Just like He tells us to look for a way out during temptation, we should also perhaps look for the good in the trial, because then we will be encouraged and strengthened to know that God is working on our behalf. Let me encourage you to start looking for that good, even if it seems strange. (If, at this point, finding good makes your stomach turn, then move on past this chapter, but come back to it when you are ready.)

HOW TO JOIN GOD IN WORKING GOOD

I believe God wants us to follow in His footsteps—taking every trial we face, every scheme Satan has set to destroy us, and creating a different outcome by bringing good from it. God wants us to approach trials at least with the knowledge and hope that even though we are enduring this horrible trial, we know He will use it and turn something good from it. I know it seems strange, but remember, God's ways are different from ours. The good is not always immediate; it may take months, weeks, or even years for us to see the good or even accept the good that God has developed from it, but if God says He can do it, He will. Cooperate with God in turning Satan's plans against him by grabbing onto anything good, anything of beauty, and bringing it into the light.

TRANSFORMING PAIN BY COMFORTING OTHERS

Another sentiment that annoyed and aroused bitterness in me during my grief was when well-meaning friends, spiritual leaders, counselors, and even books would say, "Through your tragedy and loss, you will be able to help comfort others in their pain." My honest thought was, *I don't care if I can help others in their pain. I can't even get past my own pain. How am I supposed to help others?*

I heard it so often that I questioned God about it one night. I prayed, "God, is comforting others with my story really something You want from me? Or is this just what everyone feels who is undergoing tragedy?" And God dropped this in my spirit: *I've called all My people to this.* This wasn't just my calling; this is *everyone's* calling. God uses all of us to comfort each other. To mourn with each other. To be there for each other. In any tragedy in our lives, God wants us to allow Him not only to work it out for our good but also for others' comfort.

I thought back to those Scriptures my son had plastered on his walls. I knew one of them said something about comfort, and I went back to look at them. Amazingly, another one of the Scriptures was 2 Corinthians 1:3–4, "All praise to God, the Father of our Lord Jesus Christ. God is our merciful Father and the source of all comfort. He comforts us in all our troubles so that we can comfort others. When they are troubled, we will be able to give them the same comfort God has given us." In anything we face, in any trial, battle, or suffering we endure, we must realize we hold heart knowledge; we hold hurt knowledge of that type of trial. Through Christ, we also hold healing and restoration knowledge, and we can use it to bring comfort to others. I believe this is God's plan.

FINDING REVELATION IN THE SIFTING OF PETER

God knew I wasn't fully convinced about comforting others, so one day, He showed me something in the sifting of Simon Peter that I had never seen before. Here, Jesus approached Peter (Simon) to tell him what to expect in the sifting he was about to receive from Satan. Luke 22:31–32 (NKJV) reads, "And the Lord said, 'Simon, Simon! Indeed, Satan has asked for you, that he may sift you as wheat. But I have prayed for you, that your faith should not fail; and when you have returned to Me, strengthen your brethren.'"

Jesus then went on to tell Peter how he would deny Him three times before the rooster crowed. What always seems to be brought out in this story of Peter is his denial of Christ, but what I saw, clear as day, were two important ideas. Let's look closer.

Jesus told Peter about this sifting before it happened. But Jesus didn't seem to worry. He informed Peter that He had already pleaded for him in prayer. Meaning? Jesus had made an intense, likely emotional argument on behalf of Peter. What is so unique about that? It doesn't say that Jesus would pray for Peter to be delivered *from* the trial. Instead, what did He pray for? That Peter's faith would not fail *through* the trial. This lets us know two things. First, that God doesn't always intend to *deliver* us from our trials, but Jesus does promise He is right there with us *in* the trial. Second, this lets us know that this trial that Peter was about to undergo was strong enough that it would even test Peter's faith. The loss of my son tested me in every way possible. It tested my desire to keep living. It was the first trial that truly ever *tested* my faith.

Even more interesting, God went on to show me what Jesus told Peter to do *after* his trial. Jesus went on to tell Peter, "But as soon as Satan is done with you, I want you to strengthen your brothers and sisters." Wait! What? After likely one of the worst tests of Peter's life, he is told to go comfort his brothers and sisters *right afterward*. Why would Jesus suggest that? Why would Jesus ask Peter to go comfort *others* after his trial?

Jesus knew that, through this trial, Peter would be stronger. So much so that *Peter would be ready to strengthen others.* Yes, Jesus knows there is value in the sifting, that it produces strength, perseverance, and character.

What an amazing Savior. Not only did He take on all our sins and suffer and die for us to give us eternity, but then He is here with us every step of the way, advocating for us and strengthening us through the trials He has already suffered and mastered.

Satan tried his best to sift our family as wheat. He hoped that no true seed of faith remained in our family. But he was sadly mistaken. Not only did we come back, but we came back swinging. Not only were we not destroyed, but we have been strengthened to comfort others. Strengthened in God's ways.

I hope that as a believer, you can see that your pain, too, can be transformed. Part of the reason it's important to share our story is that our pain can be transformed into something of value through comforting others. If I listen to God and comfort others as I have been comforted, then I complete the healing God started in me. Passing on the comfort is like the last step that never has to end. It continues to pass on from one brother or sister to another.

TRANSFORMING YOUR PAIN THROUGH REMEMBRANCE

I started to notice that focusing on remembering and honoring my lost loved one transformed my pain, as well. Remembrance of our loved ones and all the good times we've shared can bring value to our present life. When we can get our focus off of how they died and instead focus on the big, beautiful life they lived, we can transform our pain into the realization of the richness we were blessed with. We can take joy in realizing we are likely better people for having known and loved someone so special.

As suicide grievers, part of the stigma of suicide comes in the insinuation that our loved one isn't deserving of or worth remembering due to the way they died. In the same way, grievers of suicide need to realize they have the permission and right to grieve; we also need to see that we have the permission and right of remembrance and honoring our lost loved one's life. It, too, can help us transform our pain.

Remembrance of our lost loved ones in a "conventional loss" is expected, honored, and given reverence. Yet loved ones who die by suicide seem to carry an insinuated shame at every mention of their name, every photo that surfaces, and in every situation in which they are brought up. Some of this shame may be falsely perceived by us or truly insinuated by others, but either way, we must push back against this barrier to remembrance. I want all suicide grievers to feel they can freely remember their loved one just like any other lost loved one. I want suicide grievers to take back their remembrance! To feel they can show the same love, honor, and pride they would have shown had their loved one died *any other way*.

Besides, true remembrance is about celebrating a life well lived, not about focusing on how someone passed away.

Ronald Rolhesier warns of this danger in his book *Bruised and Wounded*:

> Indeed, as part of its darkness and stigma, suicide not only takes our loved ones away from us, but it also takes away our true remembrance of them. The gift that they brought to our lives is no longer celebrated. We never again speak with pride about their lives. Their pictures come off the wall, their photos of them get buried deep inside drawers that we never open again, their names are less and less mentioned in conversation, and of the manner of their death, we rarely speak. Suicide takes our loved ones away from us in more ways than we sometimes admit.[3]

We, as suicide grievers, have every right to remember our loved ones with fondness, to bring them up as much as anyone else would bring up their lost loved one. We have a right to be proud of their lives, proud of the positive impact they made through their actions, values, and accomplishments. I want all grievers of suicide to have the freedom to speak of their loved ones with pride. So, what can we do to accomplish this? If you are a suicide griever, don't be afraid to remember your loved one in any way you want. If you are *not* a suicide

---

3. Rolheiser, *Bruised and Wounded*, 9.

griever, allow suicide grievers to bring up their loved one's name without bringing an awkward silence or an uncomfortable air.

One thing I have set out to do is honor my son's life, and I pray that you feel led to honor your lost loved one in meaningful ways, as well. I want to honor my son and remember him for the rest of *my* life. Following are some of the meaningful ways, both big and small, that we have honored and remembered our son and brother. Perhaps you would enjoy doing something similar for your lost loved one.

- Light a candle. At family gatherings, we burn memory candles with Haden's picture and the words: *In Loving Memory of Robert Haden Myers, Always in Our Hearts.*
- On his birthday, we do things he loved to do, like hunting and ministering to others.
- We write/journal about the memories we shared of our son and brother.
- We are advocates for the awareness of depression and death by suicide. (We participate in suicide prevention walks, share on social media about mental health awareness, etc.)
- We wear his clothes.
- We had a memory blanket made from all his T-shirts and pajama pants.
- We set up a special shelf in our home that holds a picture and a few special mementos to remember him by. (I'd suggest you make a shelf for all your children.)
- We made sure to collect and safely store all pictures/videos, etc., that we could find.
- We had a memorial tree gifted to us by friends. We decorate it at Christmas and had a plaque made in his honor to sit below it.
- We kept his truck to give to his little brother when he can drive.
- To preserve his handwriting, we created necklaces, chains, and rings featuring his handwriting, lifted from cards he had signed to each of us over the years.

- My sister in love, who had lost her son the year before, was thoughtful enough to have my son's fingerprints taken on the day of the viewing, and I now have a necklace with my son's fingerprints on it.
- As believers, we realize Haden is still in our future, not just our past.
- We accept joy and laughter in whatever form it happens.
- We choose to live life to the fullest. For example, my daughter pursued her dream of barrel racing and horsemanship and now dedicates each event to remembrance of her brother.

HOW A RELATIONSHIP WITH CHRIST CAN TRANSFORM PAIN

God and Satan are both on the lookout for our pain, but they both have very different objectives. Satan wants to find any pain, any weakness we have, and use it as a foothold to get into our lives. He is looking to kill, steal, and destroy. Satan hopes to get us so hung up on our pain and weakness and so blinded and defeated by it that we end up turning from God.

God, on the other hand, has far greater intentions for our pain and weaknesses. His motives include using our weaknesses and trials as opportunities to display His strength, and He promises to use any trials we have in our lives for good, to redeem any pain we must endure.

I hope you have found that you, too, can transform your pain into something of value. Something that helps you more fully appreciate the treasure you had in your loved one.

Jesus, who willingly chose to suffer and die to not only conquer death but also give us the gift of eternal life, knows more than anyone how pain can end in purpose. He suffered the greatest amount of pain ever known, but He also ushered in the greatest purpose from that pain. As Christ's followers, we, too, can usher in purpose from our pain. Not that it makes the pain easier, but at least, it ends in something other than just pain. Our pain can usher in good, our pain can end in comforting others, and our pain can bring remembrance and honor to our lost loved ones. Praise God that He can take the ugliest things in this life and transform them. Thank God that we can, too.

Dear Lord,

I don't understand why this had to happen. I don't understand how You could ever bring good from it, but You say You will. Help me to see hope in this utter devastation. Help me to understand how good can come from my tragedy. Help me to not work against You but cooperate with You in bringing about good.

I don't understand Your ways; most of the time, they seem opposite to my ways. But I trust You. Right now, I can't imagine that I have anything that can comfort someone else, but You know what I need. Guide me in this, Lord. Let me see opportunities to love on and build up others, only when I am ready for this step. Empower me because right now, I feel powerless.

Lord, help me to transform this pain by remembering and honoring my lost loved one. Help me to make sure I spend more time and energy focusing on and recalling my lost loved one's big, beautiful life than I spend on how they passed. Thank You, God, for blessing me with my loved one.

In Jesus's mighty name, amen.

CHAPTER 7

YOUR ROAD TO
HEALING AND HOPE

Each day we give in to our grief is
one less day we give to the people we care about.
Each day lived in the past is one less day to build a future.
Each day of despair is one less day of joy.
Each day consumed by anger is one less day to love.[1]
—Margaret Brownley

For me, healing from grief *has not* been a point that I've reached but more a path that I have chosen. It's not a matter of doing X, Y, and Z to be fully healed. Grief is truly a pilgrimage that is different for everyone, although some pitfalls can prevent people from ever healing. In addition, there are likely many factors that determine your healing process, such as the age of and the closeness to the loved one that passed, the circumstances that surrounded their passing, and your faith.

In this chapter, I will share what the healing process may look like, but first, it may help to share what healing *isn't*. Healing doesn't mean the tears will forever stop, nor does it mean your heart will not ache

---

1. Margaret Brownley, *Grieving God's Way* (Tennessee: Thomas Nelson, 2012), 190.

because your loved one isn't here with you. It doesn't mean you won't consider what those future events would have looked like if your loved one were here. It doesn't mean in those quiet moments of remembrance you won't sob and ache in longing for them. And it doesn't mean you won't think about them, potentially, every single day of your life.

It's been years since I've lost my son, but I still experience all of these. Yet, I do believe I am on the right path. I know where my hope lies. I believe my Lord has an amazing plan for my whole family's eternity, and I know that I must stay on the path marked *Rescue* to reach the final destination marked *Glory*. There, I know beyond a shadow of a doubt we will *all* be fully *healed*.

HOW DO YOU KNOW WHEN YOU ARE HEALED?

At some point on my grief journey, I started to wonder: *Is healing even possible? And if so, what would it even look like when it came?* I even questioned my counselor about it, and she said, "You will know you are on the road to recovery when the thoughts and feelings don't master you. When you are not thinking about Haden twenty-four seven. When the crying isn't as often, not as deep, not as long. When you are back to life, enjoying the things you once did. When you can see your future without him, and it doesn't cripple you." (It took a long time—in fact, it took years—for these things to come about in my situation.)

Margaret Brownley in *Grieving's God's Way* suggests another example of what healing looks like: "When we stop asking God why and start asking for strength and guidance, we know we are healing. When we stop praying with closed fists and start reaching out to heaven with open hands, we know we are healing. When our loss stops commanding all the attention and life becomes more God-centered, we know we are healing." [2]

David Biebel, in his book *If God Is So Good, Why Do I Hurt So Bad?*, explains the path of healing this way:

---

2. Ibid., 194.

- When I'm able to think of the person with joy instead of a nagging feeling of anguish. When my mind is no longer controlled by remorse, anger, or a need for revenge.
- When I can ask questions other than those unanswerable ones that begin with "why." When my day is not filled with statements that begin with "if only."
- When you begin to be willing to risk loving again, knowing far better than before the painful potentialities in that choice.[3]

It took a long while before I could thank God for having blessed me with my son because the grief was so thick, I couldn't see through it. But as the intensity of the grief dissipated, I could see how beautifully blessed I had been for those twenty years. It is so hard to turn that corner from the bitterness of loss into the realization of thankfulness for what we were blessed with, but once you reach that place on the path of grief, life starts to take on beauty again. We can truly be thankful for what we were given, even if what we were given was only ours for a short time. I'd say once we reach this fork in the road and we take the path of thankfulness, we are heading toward healing. For me, healing from grief doesn't mean it's no longer painful. Healing doesn't mean you forget about it. Being on the road to healing means you are choosing to move forward—not move on, but move forward. When your healing is progressing, you can see that there is still beauty in life. You know that you can experience joy. You know other loved ones need you. Your smile doesn't seem quite so scarred, and your laugh doesn't feel quite so apprehensive.

WE EACH HAVE RESPONSIBILITY IN HEALING

I felt I had a responsibility to heal—a responsibility to make sure I did everything I could to grieve well. But I suppose my husband and other children felt that *they* had a responsibility to heal, as well. It has to do with knowing that if you don't heal well, you may very well either

---

3. Biebel, *If God Is So Good,* 169.

perish from grief or, at the very least, add more heartache and pain to your loved ones because they see you aren't making it.

In the same way, if we heal well and realize this trial has made us stronger, others will perhaps be strengthened. Otherwise, they too may lose heart if they see us destroyed after our trial. Don't misinterpret this—it's not a matter of *looking* healed or *acting* healed, it's a matter of taking the right steps to *truly* heal well.

In the same way that we cannot live off someone else's faith, we also cannot live off someone else's healing from grief. If you are living through tragedy and you've watched your loved one be restored by God, you cannot live off of their healing. You must find that peace and restoration for yourself.

We don't want the legacy of our lost loved one to end with our stagnant grief, bitterness, and depression. To honor their legacy, we should strive to do all we can to heal, live our lives to the fullest, and show that although we wanted them here much longer, we can focus on realizing how precious our memories with them are.

HEALING DOESN'T MEAN YOU FORGET YOUR LOVED ONE

I felt guilt as I realized I was starting to heal. I was worried. *Well, if Haden sees me from Heaven, is he thinking, "They didn't care much for me since they've already moved on with their lives."* But I had to remember that Haden loved us, and he knew that we loved him. He would want what was best for us, and being stuck in grief the rest of our lives would not be good for anyone. Your loved one likely has the same mindset about you. Perhaps one thing you can do is ask yourself, "Are my choices or actions acting as a healthy tribute to my lost loved one?"

"One way to get beyond this is to imagine what that person (your lost loved one) might say to you. It might be something like this: 'Be happy. It's okay. You've been sad long enough.'"[4] Friend, can you hear your lost loved one saying those words to you? I realized any desire to remain in grief, even after I *felt* healing happening, was a misplaced desire to hold on to Haden. In some way, I felt that if we became

---

4. Biebel and Foster, *Finding Your Way*, 30.

healed, it meant people would stop talking about him. Stop crying over him. Stop remembering him. Stop...loving him. This is part of why we may not want our grief to end—because we don't want to say everything is okay now. It will never be *okay* that your lost loved one is gone from your present life. The pain of your loss will continue to rear its ugly head for quite possibly the rest of your life. And it's hard to imagine that. It was hard to imagine that I would be without my son for twenty, thirty, or even forty years. It was just too much to process. But even with those thoughts, I had to admit that my amazing son has most certainly become an added hope for our eternity. I pray you, too, can find that hope. One way may be in finding the value of eternity, realizing the *gift* of Heaven.

You may be reading this and thinking, *I'm not sure of my loved one's position with God*. Please realize that no matter how much we know someone, we do not have absolute certainty that a person has refused to trust in Christ all the way to the point of death. I'm sure that, just like the thief who was dying on the cross next to Christ, one's impending death will often bring a genuine heart change toward God and genuine repentance. This is between them and God; we do not know. Further, God's grace surpasses our understanding.

HEALING FROM HEAVEN

If we allow it, healing can also come in finding the peace of Heaven. First Thessalonians 4:13 reads, "And now, dear brothers and sisters, we want you to know what will happen to the believers who have died so you will not grieve like people who have no hope." This Scripture is supposed to be hopeful and helpful. In all honesty, during my loss, in my bitterness, I looked at this Scripture, and it felt offensive. It felt almost as if it was saying, "Oh, you're a believer. Well good, you don't really grieve! You'll be fine!" But as I *healed*, I started to see that this Scripture was *not lying*. If I *had* possessed a greater understanding of the hope of Heaven, perhaps I wouldn't *have felt* so offended by this verse.

Don't get me wrong; I'm not saying a Christian's loss isn't hard. I'm not saying we don't grieve, because we do (see Genesis 50:1; Lamentations 3:31–33; Matthew 5:4). And I'm not saying our loss can't vie for our faith. However, before we jump to conclusions and assume error in God's Word, we must first see if *we* line up with it, not the other way around. (Remember from chapter 4 that our feelings can be based on misinformation because of how we are interpreting our current circumstances.) So, if this Scripture is true, why did I feel the way I did? Could it be true that I didn't fully understand or appreciate the hope I have in Heaven? The hope of what my son, as a believer, might be experiencing? Could it mean that the more we see and understand our hope as believers, the more we *can* lay down that grief?

I came to realize that if we don't appreciate the gift of Heaven, we *are* bound to grieve like an unbeliever. A profound aspect of my healing came from learning about Heaven and what my son may be experiencing there. This life on earth is *not* our final experience. "Your life on this earth is a dot. From that dot extends a line that goes on for all eternity."[5] While on this earth, we live *in* the dot. When we pass on to Heaven, we live *in* that line that goes on forever. Which should mean more to us? Where should our hope be placed?

Like many believers, I used to understand very little about our eternal hope. But as I began to learn about Heaven, it became a *vital* part of my healing. In that first month after our loss, I had a friend on social media send me a list of Scriptures that answered some questions concerning our loved one's soul after death. I didn't even realize how badly I needed to *know* those answers. Or how much comfort knowing those aspects of Heaven would bring. With that realization, I started scouring the Scriptures for more answers. I did find some, but it wasn't until a few years after our loss that I stumbled upon the perfect short read that gave me my greatest insights into Heaven, Randy Alcorn's insightful book *In Light of Eternity: Perspectives on Heaven*. His insights are backed up by Scripture. These were insights I could take hope in. Following are some of his chapter titles: "What Will We Be Like in Heaven?," "The Opposite of Boredom," "Will We Remember our Lives

5.   Randy Alcorn, *In Light of Eternity: Perspectives on Heaven* (Colorado: Waterbrook Press, 1999), 143.

on Earth?," "Can Those in Heaven See What Happens Here?," and "Refreshing Rest, and the Fascinating Labor of Heaven."

Here is a small snapshot of some perspectives of Heaven that I found particularly comforting. While not every Bible scholar would agree on these points, at least, it gives us something to think on, hope for, or study on regarding Heaven. As Christ's followers, death is not an end to life but rather a new beginning for life in eternity, at which time we experience the fullness of life (2 Corinthians 5:4). Further, God's Word shares the sentiment and even excitement we should have concerning Heaven. We know that when we go to Heaven, we will no longer be in a place that has death, mourning, crying, or pain (Revelation 21:4). In fact, some even believe that, much like the beggar's experience in Luke 16:22, at the point of our passing, angels will usher our souls into Heaven. We enter into what Jesus Himself called "paradise" (Luke 23:43). Think of this: we have been invited to our Heavenly Father's home (John 14:2). Heaven is something that Paul declares as "far better" (Philippians 1:23) than this earthly experience. Further, it is a real place (John 14:2). "He *did not* say, 'I go to an indescribable realm devoid of physical properties, where your disembodied spirit will float around, and which is nothing at all like what you've ever thought of as a home.'"[6] Moreover, we will indeed be with our loved ones who have passed in Christ (1 Thessalonians 4:17). What's more, when we die, our souls will immediately enter into the presence of the Lord. Paul says it this way: "Yes, we are fully confident, and we would rather be away from these earthly bodies, for then we will be at home with the Lord" (2 Corinthians 5:8). At death, we are fully conscious of our experience and able to think, feel, speak, and recall memories. The story in Luke 16 (the rich man's conscious awareness after death) helps us see this truth. Further, many stories in the Bible let us know that we are still called by our own names in Heaven (Matthew 8:11; Luke 16:25)[7] and, more importantly, we are "still us" in Heaven (Matthew 8:11; Luke 9:30–32). We will have a temporary heavenly form (Luke 9:30–32; 2

---

6. Ibid., 12.
7. Ibid., 45.

Corinthians 5:1–4). And in that form, we still have the joy of eating and drinking (Luke 14:15; 22:14–18).

Additionally, Heaven will be a place of rest and safety (Revelation 6:11), but far from boring, as so many assume. In fact, there is great activity in Heaven, far more than just singing all day as some seem to fear. Still more, if in our lifetime on earth we can't even hope to see or experience all that this world offers in nature and beauty, imagine how much more eternity must be. There's no doubt we will be busy. We will have assigned tasks (Luke 19:17), and we've likely heard about the worshiping, celebrating, and singing, but along with that, Heaven is a place where we will still share in community with other believers (John 14:2). Randy Alcorn helps us see we might even be able to visit with anyone who has ever lived and died in Christ, because they are there in Heaven, as well. First Corinthians 2:9 says it well: "This is what the Scriptures mean when they say, 'No eye has seen, no ear has heard, and no mind has imagined what God has prepared for those who love him.'"

Oftentimes, I think we worry if we are "excited for Heaven" or "one day closer to Heaven" because that seems morbid. But as Christ's followers, it's okay to be excited for Heaven or for us to be excited about being one day closer to our lost loved ones. It's not death we are excited for, but true life. Life without suffering, trial, or pain. Life with our lost loved ones, a life seeing God face to face, walking with Him like in the Garden.

DO OUR LOVED ONES IN HEAVEN SEE ACTIVITIES ON EARTH?

Although I had heard that to some degree our loved ones in Heaven are aware of activities and events on earth, I still wondered how this could be true since they would potentially also be witnesses to the pain here. Then I found an article published by the Gospel Herald Ministries, entitled "Do Loved Ones in Heaven Look Down on Us?" which featured a Q&A from the Billy Graham Evangelistic Association. In this article, Billy Graham lets us know that although the Bible doesn't answer all our questions about Heaven, it *does* indicate that those who have already entered Heaven may be aware of events on earth. Graham is quoted as saying, "The book of Hebrews, for example, pictures life as a great arena, with those who have gone before us cheering us on in our daily spiritual struggles (see Hebrews 12:1)."

When the commentator asked, "But does this mean people in Heaven are sad when evil seems to be winning the day?" Billy answered, "No, not at all. For one thing, they (unlike us) see the whole picture; they know that even amid life's heartaches and trials, God is still working behind the scenes," he further explained. "They also know that Satan is a defeated foe, and someday all evil will be destroyed and Christ will rule in perfect peace and justice."

The article went on to share Harvest Church pastor Greg Laurie's thoughts on the issue. "People in Heaven do, in fact, have knowledge of what is happening on earth. [They] will see and understand and assess all things in a perfectly spiritual way that takes into account everything they need to know in order to make sense of it and to keep from making any mistakes," he explained. "And so, they will not in the least doubt the goodness of God in what they see or the wisdom of God in what they see."[8]

Later, I found this Scripture that convinced me that our loved ones do see what is happening, but that they can live above the fear or pain it might cause someone here on earth. That verse is 1 Corinthians 13:12 (NKJV): "For now we see in a mirror, dimly, but then face to face. Now I know in part, but then I shall know just as I also am known." Now, we see things imperfectly, like puzzling reflections in a mirror, but then we will see everything with perfect clarity. Those in Heaven can see, but because God promises there is no crying, mourning, or pain in Heaven, we know that they likely aren't disheartened by what they see. This showed me that we can only see so much now—but not the full picture. I believe that just as the theory suggests, when we get to Heaven, we won't be sad, partly because we are allowed to see the full picture and we know the victory that comes with it. I believe that in Heaven, we will know more of God's plan than we ever did on earth.

---

8. Billy Graham Evangelistic Association, "Do You Think People in Heaven Can See What We're Doing on Earth?," accessed February 18, 2023, https://billygraham.org/answers/do-you-think-people-in-heaven-can-see-what-were-doing-on-earth.

We will fully see the vapor that this life on earth is (James 4:14 NKJV). This Scripture is also a comfort when we learn that we aren't meant to understand everything here and now, but we are meant to have faith in God's plan.

When we see this complete picture, I imagine all we will be able to do is sit in awe of what He has done in our lives. All He has steadfastly brought us through. All He has been faithful in. All the Red Seas He has parted for us with the enemy at our heels. We will sit in awe and wonder at the love He has for us and the story He has written for us.

God knows every single tear we cry, so He knows our every heartache. How does He know? He was right there beside us. He knows every individual's pain. He catches every tear that falls (Psalm 56:8) when our hearts are racked with the excruciating pain that forces those tears to the surface. Perhaps He is the only One who knows. The only One who knows the relationship you had with your lost loved one, and what that loss truly means for you. He is the only One who knows how strongly that fear of death gripped you in your grief. He knows your grief, your guilt, your fear, your pain, your confusion. Not only does He know, but He has been there beside you, walking along with you in that valley of death. He not only knows your pain, but He died for that exact pain, that exact heartache, and those same tears. He died so we wouldn't need to suffer those things anymore. He died for us all to have an Eternity without any of that.

Dear Lord,

I don't know whether I even believe I can be healed. Lord, help me to find that path. I don't know if I can walk this road. I need Your strength because I have none left. Lord, help me to take hope in eternity. Help me to take hope that my loved one is there with You, more alive than ever. Lord, help me to see what a vapor this life really is. Help me to believe that eternity will outshine our wildest imaginations. Lord, thank You for sitting quietly beside me, patiently waiting, when I was too bitter even to call on You. Lord, forgive me if I have dishonored Your name in my anger. Lord, help me to rest in Your embrace. Help me to rest in my eternal hope.

Only in Jesus's name may I ask these things, amen.

PART THREE

GAINING CLARITY
AND HOPE

CHAPTER 8

SUICIDE STIGMA

BUILDING A BRIDGE TO UNDERSTANDING

*More time has been spent blaming people for suicide
than finding explanations for suicide.* [1]
—Adina Wrobleski

Regrettably, before we lost Haden, I harbored misconceptions and wrong judgments about death by suicide. When I lost my son in this devastating way, those assumptions, misconceptions, and judgments stared back at me in the mirror. My son and our family didn't match my preconceived notions at all. He was thoughtful, loving, and caring. Our family was a strong, active support system, and everyone who knew Haden loved him. I was so ignorant about suicide and mental health. So, I dove into research, counseling, and Bible study to understand suicide more clearly for what it truly is.

After our loss, I read book after book, trying to find help and healing, but I discovered conflicting views. Some of these books, written not only by professionals but even by mothers, described suicide victims in a way that did not fit the character of my son. They used words like *selfish*, *weak*, *lazy*, and even phrases like *full of hate*. These

---

1. Wrobleski, *Suicide Survivors*, 40.

sentiments did not match Haden in any way. Yet alongside the "name-calling" books that dripped with fear, abhorrence, and loathing, I also found books full of stories that shared the sweet character and demeanor of many who had lost their lives to suicide. These individuals were described as being some of the most loving, caring, thoughtful, and tenderhearted people, not full of pride or a desire to hurt others.

So how is it that there can be such extremes in the perceptions toward suicide victims? Stigmas. And I discovered these stigmas were fueled by fear—fear of losing people to suicide. The idea is that if people believe these stigmas are true, it will stop them from dying by suicide. Sadly, fear of these stigmas has very little power to overcome suicidal thoughts in individuals who have lost hope. The social behaviors that have developed as a result of these fears have only created prejudice and exclusion from society, and more pain and secrecy for those who suffer, which in turn has meant *more* death by suicide.

When people look at suicide victims and those who grieve them through stigmas, the lens of fear generates hate and abhorrence and produces extensive prejudice, misconceptions, and judgmental attitudes. These people may then consciously or subconsciously shun those who are suffering from a suicide loss. These exclusion behaviors don't just come from strangers. They can come from family and friends and may even affect how grievers and at-risk individuals are treated by professionals or the staff of social institutions.

Just hearing the word *suicide* can cause even the kindest people to react in ways that imply the victim and survivors are from an undesirable family and are worthy of condemnation, and that being near the suicide grievers may somehow pass that undesirableness onto them.[2] We experienced the reality of this. One couple we ran into weekly would literally look at us with wide-eyed fear in their eyes, as if we had something contagious, and veered to the opposite side of the hall as we passed by.

The stigmas behind these attitudes and behaviors can cause a vicious cycle that stresses, burdens, and wounds grievers of suicide

2. Ibid., 59.

even further, causing them to feel shamed and judged by others. These feelings can even stop them from seeking the help they need to walk through this complicated grief. And stigmas can push at-risk individuals away from much-needed medical care, away from counseling, and even away from God, family, and friends.

WHY WE RUN FROM AWARENESS

We want to keep suicide weird and mysterious, at arm's length, hush-hush, just that thing that only "crazy" families experience. Why? We fear suicide. It makes us feel vulnerable. Therefore, anger and avoidance stemming from this fear serve as our defense mechanisms. We don't want to know anything about suicide because then it makes it all the more real, all the more possible, something that could befall any of us. Perhaps people think the less they know about it, the less likely it is to happen to them. But that's not true. I'd venture to say, it's just the opposite; the more you know about it, the less likely it is to affect you or your loved ones. This fertile ground of fear is where the seeds of stigma are planted, and from these seeds emerge demoralization, judgment, disgrace, reproach, discrimination, and a discomfort that seeks to *punish* the causing factor in any way possible. That causing factor is anyone who is suicidal, anyone who dies by suicide, or any family or friends of those individuals. When people try to distance themselves from any talk of suicide, this negatively affects suicide prevention efforts because, for awareness to take place, there needs to be communication about suicide at all levels.

Knowing the actual truth about suicide is much more effective at preventing it. When we look at death by suicide through the lens of love, it generates empathy and grace and produces solutions full of hope. I have started to develop these as a result of becoming informed. I desire to help you find these for yourself, as well, and help you interact compassionately with people who harbor stigmas.

WHERE ARE STIGMAS BORN?

To understand stigmas, it's important to see how they have come about. Stigmas are often birthed out of historically ingrained beliefs of fear, discomfort, and misinformation. When addressing the stigma surrounding suicide, we must ask ourselves, "How do I know if what I *think* about suicide is true? Is my understanding based on research, personal experience, or education, or is it simply shaped by what I've always heard or seen?" To combat stigma, we must look at all the evidence and not resort to "what we've always seen or heard." Yet, seeing suicide through stigma is "easier" because confronting stigma requires addressing an issue we find highly uncomfortable.

The following story shares one way we may wrongly develop stigmas. But first, we need to understand the difference between a suicide attempt and an aborted suicide attempt. An attempted suicide involves someone who actually jumped, pulled the trigger, swallowed the pills, etc., and did not die, versus someone who experienced an aborted attempt, which takes place when someone stands at the ledge, holds the gun to their head, holds the pills in their hands, etc.. Still, they stopped themselves and did not follow through. Thomas Joiner, professor of psychology and author of *Myths about Suicide*, shares that those who attempt or die by suicide versus those who abort their attempts are not in the same state of mind. He uses the example of Halle Berry and her 2007 aborted suicide attempt. She backed away from suicide at the last minute because an image of her mother (or an *intact* social connection) prevented her from following through. Joiner points out that precisely because she still had these "ties she could not ignore"—or, again, intact social connections— she was not in the same state of mind as those who actually die by suicide. Joiner shares, "Many people take the intact social connections and attendant feelings of selfishness of some suicide attempters to be representative of those who die by suicide. This is a mistake because those who die by suicide have experienced rupture in their social connections. Thus, ideas like 'my mother would be distressed if I were gone' do not occur to them, not because they are selfish but because they are alone in a way that few can fathom. Rather, ideas like 'my mother will be better

off when I am gone' are primary. These are the antithesis of selfishness."[3] The fact that Halle Berry, a celebrity, went public, claiming she
felt selfish and therefore didn't follow through, helps us see why confusion and stigma can be created regarding those who die by suicide.

MENTAL ILLNESS IS A MAJOR RISK FACTOR FOR SUICIDE

Before we dive into understanding the specific historically ingrained
stigma that surrounds suicide, we must first look at the prevalence of
mental illness in suicide because it will help us to eradicate some of
this stigma. Sadly, the stigma surrounding suicide doesn't seem to
account for the distorted thinking or mental illness from which almost
all victims of suicide suffer. How do we know that nearly all victims of
suicide suffer from mental illness in some form? For over seventy years,
teams of trained professionals have conducted psychological autopsy
reports on those who die by suicide. One of the goals of a psychological autopsy is the re-creation of the mental state of the victim during
the time leading up to his or her death. Members of the team interview friends, family members, and the victim's doctors, covering a
comprehensive range of topics in the investigation, which helps them
determine whether mental illness played a part in the death.[4] The facts
are that 46 percent of people who have died by suicide were already
diagnosed with a mental health condition before their death.[5] These
psychological autopsy reports show us that an estimated 90 percent
[with some studies showing up to 95 percent] of those who die by
suicide have a mental health condition that frequently presents
through depression or substance abuse.[6] In addition, one study from
the National Institute of Health shares that 93 percent of suicide
attempters were found to be psychiatrically ill at the time of the

---

3. Joiner, *Myths about Suicide,* 43–44.
4. Jamison, *Night Falls Fast*, 31–32.
5. National Alliance of Mental Health, "Risk of Suicide," accessed https://www.nami.
org/About-Mental-Illness/Common-with-Mental-Illness/Risk-of-Suicide.
6. L. Meyers, "World Mental Health Day Emphasizes the Link Between Suicide and
Mental Illness, *Monitor on Psychology*, 37 (no. 11), https://www.apa.org/monitor/dec06/
healthday.

commission of the suicide attempt.[7] Finally, according to the Suicide Awareness Voices of Education, 80 to 90 percent of those who are suicidal can be helped with medication.[8] These statistics highlighting the prevalence of mental health issues related to suicide, along with the effectiveness of medication, help us to see that suicide is often linked to underlying illness.

As Christians, it's important to remember that our mental and emotional health matter deeply to God. Pastor Levi Lusko points this out beautifully: "Jesus told us to love God not just with our soul but with our heart, mind, and strength. That means our emotional and mental health are just as important to God as our spiritual health."[9] This truth Lusko shares is what Jesus shares in Luke 10:27 (NIV), when He tells us to "love the Lord your God with all your heart and with all your soul and with all your strength and with all your mind." God is not only concerned about our spiritual health, but He desires wholeness for every part of us: heart, soul, mind, and body.

What's more, I found it encouraging to learn that the American Psychiatric Association is considering creating a diagnosis of "suicidal behavior disorder."[10] This would acknowledge suicide as a distinct treatable condition rather than just a symptom of other mental health disorders. This change could be a positive step because it would provide greater access to medical help for those plagued by suicidal thoughts, it may harbor a shift in how individuals view suicide, and it would work to eradicate the idea that it is just a rash choice or an impulsive action, and that healing is possible with the right care.

THE STIGMA THAT DYING BY SUICIDE IS SIN

Throughout this book, we've looked at the reality of mental illness

---

7. National Institute of Health, "Decriminalization of Suicide as Per Section 115 of Mental Health Care Act 2017," https://pmc.ncbi.nlm.nih.gov/articles/PMC5914247/.
8. Suicide Awareness Voices of Education (SAVE), Suicide Prevention Training: An Online Resource, accessed February 21, 2025, https://www.save.org.
9. Levi Lusko, *Blessed Are the Spiraling* (Nashville: W Publishing Group, 2024), 70.
10. National Library of Medicine, "Suicidal Behavior Disorder as a Diagnostic Entity in the DSM-5 Classification System: Advantages Outweigh Limitations," https://pmc.ncbi.nlm.nih.gov/articles/PMC4102277/.

being prevalent in suicide victims. So if, as science claims, many who die by their own hand are ill, we must ponder: If it is truly the result of an illness, would God at the same time see it as sin? Again, I'm not here to tell you what to believe, but I am here to help you look at all the possibilities.

Throughout history, many of the world's prominent religions have condemned death by suicide, holding to the idea that suicide is a sin against God. Some religions have taught that God will never forgive a person who dies by suicide and that they will burn in hell for eternity. Because of this, religious leaders have been known to refuse to officiate the funerals of victims of suicide or refuse the same religious rites afforded others who died in a more "natural" manner. I read multiple stories in which suicide grievers were told, "Your loved one is burning in hell," and those who survived attempted suicide heard things like, "You'd better be glad you survived, or you would be burning in hell right now." These stigmas appear to be attempts at preventing people from dying by suicide. Still, they can easily backfire and give at-risk individuals another reason to lose hope, leading to the very deaths these ideas were supposed to prevent.

While the Roman Catholic Church is one religious body that still teaches that suicide is a sin against God, it has recanted its former stance that it is the "unforgivable sin" and that victims of it go directly to hell. In more recent history, the Roman Catholic Church has recognized that mental illness and other factors play a role in death by suicide and has stated that God can provide an opportunity for those who have died by suicide to repent and that the conditions leading up to suicide can decrease the responsibility of the victim.[11]

Unfortunately, the stigma of hate, prejudice, and fear of victims of suicide going directly to hell and having no opportunity for forgiveness continues to linger and perpetuate. This stigma comes from man-made tradition and not from the Word of God. It tells us something about

---

11. Catechism of the Catholic Church, paragraphs 2282 and 2283, accessed February 1, 2025, https://www.vatican.va/content/catechism/en/part_three/section_two/chapter_two/article_5/i_respect_for_human_life.html.

the validity of a religious belief when it can be retracted by new scientific information.

What does the Holy Bible say about suicide? Not much. There are several instances when people despaired of life in the Bible and seven incidents of death by suicide in the Bible: Abimelech (Judges 9:54), Samson (Judges 16:30), Saul (1 Samuel 31:4), Saul's armor-bearer (1 Samuel 31:5), Ahithophel (2 Samuel 17:23), Zimri (1 Kings 16:18), and Judas (Matthew 27:5). Further, someone could argue that Jonah's jumping out of a boat in the middle of the ocean could be considered a suicide attempt. Yet, these incidents in the Bible of someone dying by their own hand aren't specifically addressed as sin; further, the victims and the grievers were not made a spectacle of. And while many of these men weren't highly regarded, Saul was still honored, mourned, and treated as a war hero by David, and Samson was still included in the Hebrew faith Hall of Fame (Hebrews 11). Don't misinterpret, I am in no way saying death by suicide is condoned by God, but rather I am acknowledging that as we study the stories of those who died by suicide, there is no extreme punishment, judgment, or public humiliation used anywhere in the Bible. And although we can surmise that death by suicide is something God would never want anyone to suffer, there is no particular Scripture in God's Word that either condemns or condones death by suicide.[12]

Some would argue that the sixth commandment, "Thou shalt not kill," applies to suicide. But as doctor of ministry David Biebel sees it,

> The true meaning of any biblical text is not determined by what we want it to mean; it is understood by trying to discern the author's original intention, considering the context in which the text occurs. In this case [suicide], God, through Moses, most likely is forbidding the Israelites to take the law into their own hands by murdering their neighbors, whether in revenge or for any other reason. Surely this command was not a general prohibition against killing anyone, since

12. Biebel and Foster, *Finding Your Way*, 123.

the Israelites, with God's blessing, killed plenty of enemies after they received the commandments. Nor does it apply to suicide.[13]

Thankfully, almost all major religions have softened in their understanding of death by suicide and now seem to take into account the medical community's findings that mental health issues generally bring on suicide. Despite existing stigmas, all the major religions— including Judaism, Catholicism, Islam, Buddhism, and Hinduism—have established extensive outreach programs to at-risk individuals.[14] Some Christian denominations have even established mental health hotlines specifically for their spiritual leaders. This shows not only progress in our understanding of suicide, but it also shows that suicide can affect *anyone*.

Perhaps you still fear that suicide is a sin and wonder if it has prevented your loved one from entering God's presence. Let me assure you, God's grace, for believers, is adequate for even that last act. Even if suicide were a sin, when Jesus paid for our sins, it was an eternal act that was fully sufficient.[15] God's forgiveness is not limited by time. When we receive God's forgiveness through His Son, Jesus Christ, He forgives all the sins we have committed or will ever commit. God's grace is enough!

THE STIGMA THAT DYING BY SUICIDE IS A CRIME

Throughout history, many places in the world have enacted laws to make suicide illegal and to make those who die by suicide "criminals." This has often been thought to help prevent suicide, but legal penalties and the fear of incarceration can worsen feelings of hopelessness, guilt, and shame for those suffering from suicidality. When we use legal penalties to "prevent" suicide, we are focusing more on punishment than on prevention. This should not be. Suicide is not a moral or criminal issue but rather a mental health issue that needs medical care.

---

13. Ibid.
14. Beth Daly, "Why Religions of the World Condemn Suicide," *Conversation*, June 12, 2018, https://theconversation.com/why-religions-of-the-world-condemn-suicide-98067.
15. Romans 6:9–10.

Thankfully, in recent decades, many countries have come to decriminalize suicide and suicide attempts due to the understanding that it is a mental health issue. Further, after the decriminalization, many of these places witnessed a drop in suicide or an increase in those seeking help. In the United States, suicide was finally decriminalized when the last state, California, took it off its legal books in 1976. Unfortunately, there are still a few countries today that maintain it is a criminal act with penalties for suicide or attempted suicide.

Criminalizing death by suicide also contributes to prejudice, exclusion, and discrimination by those who are ignorant about mental health issues and suicide prevention.[16] Laws don't stop people from dying by suicide, but they do stop people from getting help at the time they most need it and receiving the kind of support that can prolong their lives. For example, in 2020, a campaign in the Cayman Islands reported that because suicide was illegal, only 5 percent of children and young people suffering from distorted thinking and mental illness were trying to get help. Yet one in three children surveyed reported suicidal ideation. This campaign asserted that suicide is never a crime and always a mental health issue. Thankfully, that December, suicide was decriminalized in the Cayman Islands, preventing this deterrent for those seeking help.[17] Today, we see many organizations (the American Foundation for Suicide Prevention, Mental Health America, the Suicide Prevention Resource Center, the World Health Organization, etc.) that advocate for the decriminalization of suicide and help others to see why it is so counterproductive.

The stigma that victims of suicide are criminals and the grievers are guilty by association does a great deal of harm and is at least partly responsible for the deaths of many precious lives. If you are in a country where you influence the laws that are made, take action to decriminalize death by suicide and instead provide help and support for those who are suffering.

---

16. Daly, "Why Religions of the World Condemn Suicide."
17. Alex Panton Foundation, "Decriminalising Suicide?," accessed February 21, 2024, https://alexpantonfoundation.ky/decriminilising-suicide/.

THE STIGMA THAT DYING BY SUICIDE IS A CHOICE

For many who die by suicide, it is not simply a choice, but the result of overwhelming psychological pain and, in many cases, a serious mental health condition. Ronald Rolheiser, a Catholic priest, internationally known speaker, and author, explains it well: "Suicide is still perhaps the most misunderstood of all deaths. We still tend to think that because it is self-inflicted, it is voluntary in a way that death through physical illness or accident is not." He goes on to emphasize, "As I have said, for most suicides, this is not true. A person dying of suicide dies, as does the victim of a physical illness or accident, against his own will."[18]

The idea that suicide is purely a choice can be appealing because it creates the illusion of control—if suicide is a choice, then a person can choose otherwise. But this oversimplification can lead to blame, whether toward those struggling or toward the loved ones left behind. It's often easier to assign blame than to confront the deeper, more painful realities surrounding suicide.

For someone to make a rational choice, their thoughts must be fully rational. However, when a person is battling a mental illness or experiencing severe psychological distress, their brain is not always functioning in a way that allows for clear thinking. Clinical psychologist Sally Spencer-Thomas explains:

> The idea of choice or free will is often discouraged when talking about suicide because thinking is often very impaired at the time of death. Sometimes, individuals in the throes of unimaginable emotional pain are not entirely capable of making a rational decision because their depression, addiction, or other mental health condition often prevents them from generating alternative solutions to their problems.[19]

John Ackerman, a clinical psychologist specializing in behavioral health and suicide prevention, states, "Intense emotional pain, hope-

---

18. Rolheiser, *Bruised and Wounded*, 23.
19. Sally Spencer-Thomas, "Language Matters: Why We Don't Say 'Committed Suicide,'" IRMI, September 15, 2021, https://www.irmi.com/articles/expert-commentary/language-matters-why-we-dont-say-committed-suicide.

lessness, and a narrowed, negative view of the future interferes with balanced decision-making. A person may believe they are making the best decision among their options, but it certainly isn't reflective of all possible choices."[20]

Additionally, many suicide attempt survivors have described experiencing what felt like intrusive, commanding thoughts urging them to end their lives—almost like hallucinations.[21] This is easy to believe, as many individuals suffering from depression or other mental illnesses battle relentless, irrational self-hatred and distorted beliefs about themselves and others. It only stands to reason that, in some cases, these lies and overwhelming emotions could intensify to the point that a person's illness seems to push them toward suicide.

No one with a healthy mind would choose to have an illness, just as no one with a healthy mind would want to die by suicide. When we reduce suicide to a matter of choice, we risk misjudging the character of those who have died, filtering our grief through misplaced blame rather than understanding.

Recognizing that suicide is often the result of intense psychological suffering rather than a simple choice allows us to honor those we have lost and bring peace to those grieving. It also fosters awareness and empathy, helping to dismantle the stigma that causes so many at-risk individuals to suffer in silence.

THE STIGMA THAT DYING BY SUICIDE IS SELFISH

The view that all suicide is a rational choice morphs into the belief that death by suicide is selfish. *Selfishness* is defined as "seeking or concentrating on one's own advantage, pleasure, or well-being without regard for others."[22] "Dying by suicide does not generate pleasure, advantage, or well-being. People who take their own lives commonly

---

20. John Ackerman, "Don't Say It's Selfish: Suicide Is Not a Choice," Nationwide Children's Hospital, November 15, 2019, https://www.nationwidechildrens.org/family-resources-education/700childrens/2019/11/suicide-is-not-a-choice.

21. Spencer-Thomas, "Language Matters: Why We Don't Say 'Committed Suicide.'"

22. "Selfish," *Merriam-Webster.com Dictionary*, Merriam-Webster, accessed February 27, 2024, https://www.merriam-webster.com/dictionary/selfish.

feel like a burden to others or experience intense emotional pain that overwhelms their capacity to continue with life. Making others feel guilty is typically the furthest thing from their mind."[23]

Having had a front-row seat to my son's life, I would say he was one of the most *selfless* people I knew. He would never do anything to hurt anyone. Dying by suicide wasn't a selfish act but a desperate act to end his pain. Sadly, I read story after story of individuals who had died by suicide who were some of the most caring people others had ever met. Ronald Rolheiser, Catholic priest, says it well in his book *Bruised and Wounded*: "Many of us have known victims of suicide, and we know, too, that in almost every case that person was not full of pride, haughtiness, and the desire to hurt anyone."[24]

One young man, Drew, who tried to end the pain of his longtime depressive episodes by jumping from a bridge, said, "I've never bought the idea that suicide is a selfish thing. To me, if the person were selfish, he wouldn't try to kill himself because he would be thinking self-preservation."[25]

Professor Thomas Joiner, in *Myths about Suicide*, helps us to see how assigning selfishness to suicide victims is a misplaced attribution by comparing it to people who are suffering intense physical pain. People in pain are undoubtedly focused on themselves and often behave in ways that appear rash and may harm others. However, their reactivity and violence are attributed to pain-induced desperation, not the idea that they are selfish individuals.[26] In the same way, the actions of those who die by suicide are caused by emotional-pain-induced and mental-pain-induced desperation. This pain-induced self-*centeredness* is brought on by distorted thinking or mental illness.

Rachel was someone who struggled with intense depression and suicidal ideations and described her experience as having blinders on because of the intense, suffocating, emotional pain. She said her ability

---

23. John Ackerman, "Don't Say It's Selfish: Suicide Is Not a Choice."
24. Rolheiser, *Bruised and Wounded*, 20.
25. Cox and Arrington, *Aftershock*, 42.
26. Joiner, *Myths about Suicide*, 47.

to perceive was so skewed that she could not see anything apart from what she herself was experiencing.[27]

Please understand that this self-centeredness does not stem from selfishness but from intense pain. Imagine having a leg chopped off—you'd be pretty self-centered at the time. When the pain is so intense and you are desperate to relieve it, you can't see anyone or anything else. This is the ground on which suicidal ideation grows.

Joiner explains further that what many believe to be selfishness in suicide is often quite the opposite. What does he mean? Is he saying that those who die by suicide actually consider their deaths to be a service to others? Yes. Extremely sad, but true. Often, suicidal individuals feel they are a burden to their loved ones, and that their loved ones would be better off without them "in the way." Some who take their own lives may carry the heartbreaking belief that their absence will ease the burden on those they love—that their death might somehow be more helpful than their life. And that belief becomes a primary motivation of those who die by suicide.[28] Joiner explains,

> One can understand somewhat the idea that suicide is selfish, in the sense that those left behind are often convinced that those who die by suicide did not consider the impact of their deaths. This is a terrible error. Those who die by suicide certainly do consider the impact of their deaths on others, but they see it differently—as a positive instead of a negative. They are wrong, but this is their view nevertheless.[29]

Sally Spencer-Thomas, a clinical psychologist, corroborates Joiner's findings. She says, "The mind of a suicidal person is distorted and often holds the belief that they will be lessening their burden on loved ones by no longer being around." This is, of course, a great deception. No one's loved ones would be better off without them. No one benefits when a loved one dies.

We experienced this firsthand, the lowering of self, this inability to

---

27. Rachel Bradley, interview by author, February 27, 2024.
28. Joiner, *Myths about Suicide*, 45.
29. Ibid., 44.

see one's worth. My son had turned twenty just weeks before his pass-ing. At his birthday party, he acted shocked that we would do so much for him and that we would get him the gifts we did. I remember thinking it was strange. He acted as if he wasn't worthy of that much love. His illness had likely changed his perception of his life, himself, God, and others. A selflessness that slid into a sense of worthlessness.

SHOCKING SOCIAL BEHAVIORS CAUSED BY SUICIDE STIGMAS

Few stigmas in history have inflicted more cruelty than the stigma of suicide–toward both the lost and those left behind. Some of these "prevention" tactics go beyond condemning death by suicide to vili-fying and disgracing those poor souls who are victims of it, such as refusing to place a grave marker at the place where a suicide victim is buried. This insinuates that death by suicide means the victim's whole life isn't worth remembering. Some of the most sickening behaviors have been publicly disfiguring, displaying, and mutilating the corpse of the individual who died by suicide.[30] Historically, it was common to have the corpse of a suicide victim dragged through the streets.[31] It was also common to decapitate the victim and hang their head in the town square. In some countries, the government even created policies to seize the possessions of a suicide victim, even if that meant kicking their mourning families out on the street.[32] I pray these practices are no longer alive anywhere in the world.

Thankfully, these practices are at least no longer happening in developed countries, but they serve as examples of what fear and false information can do in a society. There are still plenty of horrifying social behaviors alive today, even in the United States. In some cases, loved ones of the suicide victim aren't allowed to take part in the deceased's funeral, or the deceased isn't even allowed to have a funeral because of their manner of death. Some religious grave sites won't let a suicide victim to be buried in their cemetery at all. Many suicide

---

30. Biebel and Foster, *Finding Your Way*, 122.
31. Hsu, *Grieving a Suicide*, 112.
32. Biebel and Foster, *Finding Your Way*, 122.

grievers are not allowed to mourn by those around them, or members of their social circle infer the deceased is unworthy of being mourned. The grieving family and friends are stereotyped, shunned, shamed, avoided, and treated as if they are untrustworthy or crazy.

Sometimes the lives of those who die by suicide are not given the same honor as the lives of those who die by some other means. For example, two teens from the same high school who die in the same year might be treated very differently if one of the teens dies in a car wreck and the other dies as a result of suicide. The first teen might be honored by the school with a tree or a commemorative plaque, and the second teen might not be honored at all, solely because of how they died.

When a person survives a suicide attempt, they may be told they are cowards, weak, selfish, crazy, or an attention seeker. These types of "preventive measures" cause so much more heartache and pain on top of what the suffering person is already dealing with that they continue and contribute to the cycle of wanting to end it all. This is why it is so important to increase awareness of the truth and put an end to the harmful misinformation spread by stigmas.

How to Promote Understanding and Stop Stigmas

Now that you are informed of the truth about suicide, every time the topic comes up, you have an opportunity to educate and raise awareness of suicide prevention methods. Before I dove into my research, there were times we shared about Haden's death in very shocking and ignorant ways, obviously not out of disrespect, but out of pure ignorance of how to deal with the situation ourselves. So give yourself and others a lot of grace. Most people don't know how to talk about suicide. But the language we use matters.

You've likely already figured this out: People may be insensitive and make hurtful remarks when talking about your loved one's death. They are likely *not* intending to hurt you, but they likely don't understand the complexities of suicide loss. We had some very close friends say and do things that felt completely unsympathetic. Less than a year after our loss, we had a close friend come up and try to explain a lengthy process he had endured while traveling, which was hard for him. He literally took his hands and mocked his death in the same manner my son died. I had to turn away as my stomach lurched. Most people aren't aware of how raw and sensitive suicide grievers are. Another close friend said, "I think it was an accident. He wouldn't have been brave enough to do that." I thought, *Really? It's not a matter of being brave enough but rather being ill enough.* For me, it hurt for the longest time to even say the "S word"—*suicide*—so hearing anyone surround it with a sentence of ignorant words cut to my core that much more. Sadly, the reality is that we humans are rarely sensitive to situations we have no understanding of or experience with. Again, having grace with yourself and others is paramount at this time. While it's okay to experience emotions of hurt when situations like these happen, if you can push past them and respond with your informed compassion and knowledge, these moments can turn into opportunities to raise suicide awareness and, in turn, aid in suicide prevention efforts.

No matter who you are—someone grieving, supporting a survivor, or just having a conversation—your words carry weight when it comes to suicide. Those words can either build bridges or deepen wounds. Scripture reminds us that "death and life are in the power of the tongue" (Proverbs 18:21 NKJV), and few topics reveal the truth of that statement more than the topic of suicide. The words we use can influence not only how others feel but also whether someone in pain feels seen, heard, and safe enough to speak up.

Let's look at some of the words commonly associated with suicide and some better alternatives. From her article "Language Matters," Dr. Sally Spencer-Thomas is credited with providing most of the following insights.

The phrase "committed suicide" can be especially hurtful to suicide survivors and damaging to public understanding. As Dr. Spencer-Thomas explains, it carries the connotation of a crime or a sin—people commit murder; they commit adultery. So saying someone "committed suicide" reinforces stigma that may cause at-risk individuals to isolate and hide. Similarly, saying that someone "killed themselves" suggests a rational, deliberate choice. Dr. Spencer-

Thomas offers helpful guidance on how to reframe this type of language:

> The litmus test for talking about suicide is to substitute the word "cancer" for the word "suicide" to see if the sentence still makes sense or if it has a negative connotation. We wouldn't say "committed cancer" or "successful cancer." We would simply say "cancer death" or "died of cancer." Thus, when it comes to suicide, we should say "suicide death" or "died by suicide."[33]

Saying a suicide attempt was "successful" or "unsuccessful" implies that death by suicide is some kind of achievement instead of the tragedy it truly is.[34] Instead of focusing on the attempt itself, we should focus on the person, whether they survive or not.

Thankfully, journalists are encouraged to talk about people who died by suicide as people first, not define them by their manner of death—a practice known as safe reporting guidelines. We'd be wise to follow these guidelines in everyday conversations as well. Suicide should never be used as a noun—"the suicide was wheeled into the morgue"—because it dehumanizes the individual. We wouldn't say, "The diabetes was moved out of ICU."[35] Defining a person by their life instead of the way they died acknowledges that they were so much more than the distorted thinking or mental illness that ended their life. It is so important to me that Haden be known for who he was and not how his life ended. He deserves that. And I'm sure you would want that for your loved one, as well.

The next hurdle is people who offer unsolicited theories of why someone died by suicide. These self-important ideas potentially damage someone's legacy. And as well-meaning as a person may be, their theories are more likely to hurt the grieving family and friends than to help them. While mental illness is often a major factor, no one can fully understand all of the personal battles that lead someone to

---

33. Sally Spencer-Thomas, "Language Matters."
34. Ibid.
35. Ibid.

die by suicide. Even if the victim were able to clearly tell you a reason, their thinking is likely so distorted that what they say may not even be true or, at the least, twisted by illness. The only One who fully understands the reason someone died by suicide is God, and that is why we should wisely leave understanding and judgment in His hands.

Let me encourage you with words from the American Association of Suicidology's *SOS Handbook for Survivors of Suicide* by Jeffrey Jackson. He says, "If you encounter someone that seems determined to upset you with morbid curiosity, their own self-important theories, or some form of 'guilt trip,' simply sidestep them by saying, 'I'd rather not talk about it right now.'" Please wait until you are less raw and able to inform them with compassion and patience.

WHAT ARE EFFECTIVE DETERRENTS FOR SUICIDE?

People who understand mental illness or the nature of psychological and emotional healing can easily see why these stigmas have the opposite of their *intended* effect. However, people who are uninformed can easily confuse their own fear and condemnation with love and compassion. That's why it's important to patiently but boldly educate those who still hold on to these stigmas. Ending stigmas not only gives a voice to those who have died by suicide but it also encourages knowledge, peace, and healing for those who have lost loved ones this way.

So, what are effective deterrents for suicide? Education, awareness, empathy, open doors, and grace. Replacing stigmas and educating the public with the truth that suicide is a result of distorted thinking or mental illness can cause attitudes of inclusion, acceptance, patience, compassion, and love. This would create an environment of hope instead of the environment of shame, judgment, and despair created by the majority of deterrents used throughout history. These positive behaviors would encourage individuals who are sick to reach for the help that support groups and recovery groups provide, and they would help at-risk individuals receive the same level of care and understanding that other sick people receive.

Thankfully, as we look at the past and compare it to the present, we see we have come a long way in knowledge, understanding, and empathy regarding suicide. Even insurance companies are beginning to see that death by suicide is the result of distorted thinking and mental health issues. As a result, some have started to take a more sympathetic view toward death by suicide, and more companies than ever before are now covering the mental health issues that contribute to suicide as well as the costs of death by suicide.

But, painfully, we still have so much to learn and make right. As clinical psychologist Kay Redfield Jamison, shares in her book *Night Falls Fast*, "Certainly, public understanding of suicide has increased over recent years, although not to a degree commensurate with what has been learned from medical and psychological research. The harshness of centuries-old views of suicide still touches the present, both in social policy and in personal ways."[36] I hope to be a force for change, and you can be too.

WHAT YOU CAN DO TO STOP STIGMA AND BRING AWARENESS

The following are ways to work toward preventing suicide stigma, bringing awareness to the issue, and, in turn, preventing further deaths by suicide.

- Fight for your healing in the best way possible by turning to God and getting counseling. Be willing to forgive.
- "Raise your voice to help break down the stigma.... We can all play a part in tackling suicide stigma and discrimination and challenging suicide myths."[37]
- "Use safe, inclusive, and respectful language. The language we use plays an important role in shaping opinions and beliefs about suicide."[38]
- "Examine your thought processes and understanding. Are

36. Jamison, *Night Falls Fast*, 18.
37. SuicideLine Victoria, "Overcoming the Stigma about Suicide," Suicideline Victoria, accessed February 2, 2024, https://suicideline.org.au/mental-health/overcoming-the-stigma-about-suicide/.
38. Ibid.

they right? Could you be more sensitive around suicide stigma?"[39]

- "Show compassion for anyone who is struggling and treat people with respect."[40] Reach out to them and listen.
- "Participate in campaigns or events that challenge the stigma."[41]
- "Report any media coverage that stigmatizes suicide."[42]
- Educate yourself further on the subjects of death by suicide and mental health.
- Be willing to share about any mental health issues you have to help normalize the issue.
- Not only reassure anyone in psychological pain that help is available, but lend a hand for them to find aid.
- If someone shares their plans to die, don't keep silent! Don't promise secrecy. Don't leave the individual until you find this individual help. Call the 9-8-8 Suicide and Crisis lifeline.

Dear Lord,

I pray that the perception of suicide will be changed, and let it start with me. Help me to understand, as much as possible, where my loved one may have been on that fateful day. Help me to have forgiveness, empathy, and grace, and with that, healing.

Lord, as I move forward as a suicide griever, I pray that You will give me the wisdom in how to handle others who act or speak with ignorance about suicide. Help me to have patience and grace with them. Help me to help them understand. Give me the wisdom and words to spread the truth about suicide. I pray that communication regarding suicide will soon be commonplace and normalized so that those suffering don't have to hide or fear rejection. I ask that any shame regarding suicide be replaced with empathy and love. I pray that You give me and others the boldness to reveal suicide stigma and misinformation for what it is. Lord, foremost, help me to keep my eyes on You.

---

39. Ibid.
40. Ibid.
41. Ibid.
42. Ibid.

In Jesus's name, amen.

CHAPTER 9

SUICIDE CAN BE PREVENTED

WHAT YOU NEED TO KNOW

If the meaning of your life is lost, ask for help finding it.
—Unknown

I'd like to share the personal testimony of a dear friend, whose journey through despair and toward healing reminds us that even in our darkest moments, there is hope. His story serves as a powerful reminder that suicide can be preventable when we dare to reach out for help.

From the outside, I appeared happy, successful, and healthy. The problem was that under the surface, a different story was being told.

Raised in church, I knew right from wrong, but I always felt like I wasn't good enough. The gap between who I was and who I thought I should be filled me with anxiety, leading to addictions that would send all the noise in my head into the background. The shame and those suppressed emotions turned into depression.

In search of freedom, I chased the next thing I thought would make me happy. The problem was that each accomplishment or milestone I hit left me feeling more disappointed. I frequently thought about ending my life, but the thoughts never turned to actions—until they did.

In June 2014, I thought I had finally found the key to happiness—a Jeep Wrangler I had dreamed of owning for years. But within minutes of its delivery, the excitement faded, replaced by crushing disappointment. That night, as my family slept, I stayed up in the garage, feeling attacked by my thoughts. It was crushing to find that I felt no happiness. I was convinced I was making everyone's life as miserable as I felt. I was exhausted from the effort I put into trying to feel better.

Exhausted and hopeless, I got a gun, loaded it, and sat in the driver's seat, ready to end my pain. I put the gun to my head and prayed.

Then, a whisper saved my life.

I didn't hear God's audible voice, but I sensed a clear message: "Your solution will be her solution." I knew it referred to my three-year-old daughter, who, even at her young age, carried anxieties like mine. If I ended my life, I would be modeling suicide as an option for her future. I lowered the gun.

I didn't tell anyone what had happened that night. I went to bed at 5 a.m., woke up at 9 a.m., ate breakfast with my family, and went about my day as if nothing had changed. But six months later, my world shook again—a close friend took his life by jumping from a high-rise building downtown. I had just played golf with him weeks before. He was funny and talented and had a great family. Why didn't he tell me he was struggling? And then it hit me—I hadn't told him of my struggles either. And like my friend, no one would ever be able to tell because I was an experienced mask-wearer.

Eventually, I opened up to my wife, who hid our gun and scheduled a counseling appointment. We worked together to fight the battle. Therapy wasn't something I wanted, but I knew I needed help. Counseling helped me unpack the lies I believed and replace them with biblical truth. My counselor also helped me to see where Jesus was in each piece of my story. On top of that, I took the risk of being honest with a few close friends, and in doing so, I saw the beauty in being vulnerable about my journey. Vulnerability was no longer a weakness, but a weapon. I began confessing the things I had kept hidden, and slowly, I started healing. I believe the prayers of my wife, friends, and men's groups made a difference. I began to recognize that God was pursuing me.

At first, it felt like peeling an onion—layer after painful layer. It hurt, and it was exhausting. But then, one day, while working through a layer, I had a moment of realization: I am fully known and fully loved. The battle didn't end there, but knowing I wasn't fighting alone changed everything.

As I healed, I began noticing the pain in the men around me. I started to be intentional about creating time and an environment to open up to them and share my struggles, and in turn, they shared theirs. I would share some of the things I learned on my journey, and I could see the hope it sparked in them. I founded Mission 15:4, a nonprofit focused on helping those battling depression and anxiety. The verse that drives me is Luke 15:4 (NIV): "Suppose one of you has a hundred sheep and loses one of them. Doesn't he leave the ninety-nine in the open country and go after the lost sheep until he finds it?" I had been the one, and now I was on a mission to pursue the ones.

To anyone feeling hopeless, please know this: You are fully loved, just as you are. Help is available, and healing is possible.[1]

∼

While not every suicide is preventable, stories like his prove that prevention, whether through faith, community, or professional help, can make a difference. Unfortunately, not every loved one has that moment of pause or that whisper of hope. I know that reality all too well. Losing my son—a young man who was just starting his life—to a self-inflicted death stemming from major depression opened my eyes to things humans were never intended to see. My eyes were opened to traumatic grief. My eyes were opened to the crushing weight of major depression. My eyes were opened to how the unbelievable loss of a child decimates a parent's soul. My eyes were opened to death by suicide and, in turn, to my own suicidal urges in grief. My eyes were simply opened to so much more than I ever wanted to see.

Tragically, every forty seconds, somewhere in the world, someone loses their life to suicide.[2] This means over ninety mothers and fathers have their eyes open in this way *every single hour* of *every day*. In the hour it takes to watch one TV show, cook one meal, or mow the lawn,

---

1. Nick Nelson, interview by author, February 7, 2025.
2. "Suicide: One Person Dies Every 40 Seconds," *World Health Organization,* September 9, 2019, https://www.who.int/news/item/09-09-2019-suicide-one-person-dies-every-40-seconds.

ninety precious souls somewhere in the world were so distraught and hopeless that they took their own lives. For every person who dies, there are approximately twenty-five individuals who survive suicide attempts but do not die.[3] That's approximately 54,000 weary souls who attempt to end their lives on any given day. Yet, the reality is more devastating than we believe because suicide deaths are actually *underreported*. Many "accidents" like car wrecks, drug overdoses, etc., are not accidental at all but were used to cover up death by suicide. It's obvious that a devastating worldwide pandemic existed long before COVID-19 showed up. The shocking thing is that I was scarcely aware of it, and I'm guessing you weren't either—that is, until it came crashing through our lives.

Thankfully, though, prevention is possible. As I've noted previously, the vast majority of individuals who receive timely and appropriate care can manage or even overcome suicidality.

WHAT MAKES SOMEONE AT GREATER RISK FOR SUICIDE?

Life-threatening depression isn't always easy to spot, as I can attest to due to the nightmare our family has walked through. But you can start by being aware of the risk factors that can increase someone's vulnerability to suicide:

- chronic pain; life-altering disabilities; terminal diagnoses
- stressful life events, like major transitions, loss, divorce, rejection, bullying
- financial issues
- personal or family history of mental disorders
- substance use (legal or illegal)
- past suicide attempts
- exposure to violence, including physical or sexual abuse
- having recently been released from prison or jail

---

3. Suicide Awareness Voices of Education, "2021 USA General Statistics," https://save. org/about-suicide/suicide-statistics/.

- exposure to suicidal behavior, whether personally or in the news, etc.

In addition, several groups of people are substantially affected by suicide. Some of those include veterans or current military personnel, many of those in the LGBTQ community, the elderly, those in rural communities, and first responders (law enforcement, firefighters, and EMS providers). Shockingly, more police officers die yearly by suicide than are killed in the line of duty.

The National Institute of Mental Health webpage tells us that in the United States in 2020, suicide was the *second-leading* cause of death of children ages ten through fourteen and of adults ages twenty-five through thirty-four. It was the third leading cause of death for teens between the ages of fifteen and twenty-four. And even for adults ages thirty-five to forty-four, it was the fourth-leading cause of death.[4] Often we believe our children need us the most when they are young, but according to these statistics, they need our attentive awareness well into young and middle adulthood.

In addition, American Indians and Alaska Native youth aged 10-34 experience higher suicide rates than any other U.S. racial or ethnic group and can be more susceptible to life-threatening depression than any other people group in the United States.[5] As I've mentioned previously, another group that is at higher risk are those who suffer from dyslexia, as they are 46 percent more likely to die by suicide than the general public.

If someone is suffering from depression and suicidal ideations, whatever the contributing factor, the presence of lethal means in or near the home can increase the risk of suicide. This could include medications in lethal dosages, firearms, and nearby bridges or cliffs. If someone you know suffers from depression and is going through a

4. National Institute of Mental Health, "Suicide," accessed September 21, 2023, https://www.nimh.nih.gov/health/statistics/suicide.
5. U.S. Department of Health and Human Services, Office of Minority Health, "Mental and Behavioral Health—American Indians/Alaska Natives. Updated February 13, 2025. Accessed August 26, 202. https://minorityhealth.hhs.gov/mental-and-behavioral-health-american-indian-alaskanatives.

short-term crisis, you may be able to prevent their suicide by providing distance from any lethal means that are available to them. This is especially true for men, who generally use more lethal ways to attempt suicide, which leads to a higher number of actual deaths.[6] (Women attempt more often, but they usually use less lethal means.) While anyone of any age, race, gender, ethnicity, or socioeconomic status can be affected by suicide, these groups seem to be more severely affected.

THE IMPERFECTLY PERFECT STORM

Tragically, my son was surrounded by many of the same factors that research shows can heighten suicide risk—a heartbreaking convergence I've come to think of as an imperfectly perfect storm. He was male, a Native American, in the fifteen- to twenty-four-year-old age range who suffered from dyslexia, had a family history of depression, had access to lethal means, was newly living on his own, and was grieving from the loss of family members. In addition, he was around others who were grieving and potentially depressed. (Being around others who are depressed can exacerbate depression symptoms for someone who is already depressed and make it harder for them to recover.) As you can see, many contributing factors can be playing into suicide. If we had been able to identify Haden's depression as potentially life-threatening, we might have been able to distance him from the means to go through with it while at the same time working to feed hope into his life. I pray our restoration story can be someone's prevention story.

We must let those at risk know they are not alone, that they are *not* weak people but likely ill people, that suicide isn't the only option to end their pain, and that they *can* very likely overcome this illness.

WARNING SIGNS TO WATCH FOR

Hindsight is never more torturous than when you have lost a loved one

---

6. National Action Alliance for Suicide Prevention, "Lethal Means," accessed September 21, 2023, https://theactionalliance.org/our-strategy/lethal-means.

to suicide. Although suicide seems to come out of nowhere, it's not because there were no warning signs; it's more likely that the warning signs were not known or recognized.[7]

Often, those who die by suicide are no longer really themselves by the time they die.[8] In hindsight, Haden had started to retreat from his family. In that last year, he stopped hanging around with us as much. He stopped going on family vacations, and he stopped eating lunch with us after church, instead eating out with his friends. He also didn't hunt as much as he had in previous years. At the time, I just saw it as him growing up or trying to become his own man. I didn't realize that withdrawing from loved ones and activities was also a symptom of major depression and, ultimately, a warning sign of suicide.

Sadly, at different times, I had even noticed his withdrawal from two different sets of friends. I had questioned him, and he had given reasonable answers to why he had stopped hanging out with them, yet *now*, it felt excruciatingly frustrating to realize I'd never put these things together. Overall, I share this because you need to see that if your loved one changed into a "different person," it was likely that an illness was affecting their thinking, mood, and behavior, which ultimately affected their relationships.[9]

In his book *Grieving a Suicide*, Albert Hsu says, "Those who survive a suicide attempt may later be quite baffled at that 'other person' that they were at the time of the attempt."[10] This helped me to realize how much Haden's illness may have changed him and his personality in the end. Strangely, this gave me comfort, because I knew that if this sickness had not altered our son, we would have all likely had an even closer relationship with him.

In addition to changes in personality, those who die by suicide often attempt to communicate their suicidal thoughts to friends,

---

7. Richard B. Krueger, "Aborted Suicide Attempts: A New Classification of Suicidal Behavior," *American Journal of Psychiatry* 155, no. 3 (March 1998): 385.

8. Hsu, *Grieving a Suicide*, 75.

9. U.S. National Library of Medicine, "Mental Disorders," MedlinePlus, accessed February 2, 2024, https://medlineplus.gov/mentaldisorders.html.

10. Hsu, *Grieving a Suicide*, 91.

family, or their doctors in various ways that can easily be missed.[11] However, "most suicidal individuals rarely warn their family and friends directly; instead, they may offer vague verbal clues, usually to people who are not in a position to help."[12] Agonizingly, after our son's passing, the reality that Haden *had* communicated his thoughts to someone outside of his immediate family later became apparent in our situation, as well.

While those who die by suicide have distorted thinking, this does not mean they are dangerous to others or can't function in society. In fact, "most people who have a mental disorder are neither psychotic, demented, intoxicated, nor delirious."[13] There are numerous documented cases in which a victim of suicide seemed to be of perfectly sound mind hours or even minutes, just before their death. [14] Mental health issues can truly be sinister in their methods. "Even mental health professionals often fail to detect the warning signs of suicide."[15] This is why it is so important to raise awareness of suicide warning signs so they become common knowledge, as one small clue may help someone save a life. Once warning signs have been identified, some mental health practitioners can now use imaging technologies to discern brain patterns that suggest an increased risk of suicide. There is still much research underway concerning this, but using this technology could be extremely helpful— especially when at-risk patients aren't thinking clearly and may not even see their own symptoms, which creates a breakdown between them and their practitioner.[16]

The following are common warning signs for suicide that must be taken seriously and addressed with compassion.

- expressions of helplessness or hopelessness; statements like: "I'll just end it all," "You won't be seeing me around here

11. Kruegar, "Aborted Suicide Attempts," 385.
12. Cobain and Larch, *Dying to Be Free*, 74.
13. Joiner, *Myths about Suicide*, 89.
14. Ibid., 87.
15. Jackson, *A Handbook for Coping with Suicide Grief*, 19.
16. Hilary Blumberg, "Brain Scans as Predictors of Suicide," *Yale Medicine Magazine*, Spring 2017 2–3, www.medicine.yale.edu/news/yale-medicine-magazine/article/brain-scans-as-predictoris-of-suicide.

anymore," "No one needs me," and "Everyone would be better off without me"
- extreme withdrawal from friends, family, and usual activities, for example, sex, hobbies, or sports
- talk about feeling trapped or unbearable pain
- talk about being a burden to others
- talk about suicide
- developing risk-taking behaviors
- giving away favorite possessions
- changes in behavior or mood
- increasing use of alcohol or drugs
- identification with someone who has died by suicide
- preoccupation with thoughts of death
- clear plans to die by suicide
- previous suicide attempts
- extreme mood swings
- sudden mood improvement after prolonged, consistent depression[17]

This last warning sign can be especially deceptive. Only in *hindsight* did we see the calm before the storm. Often, those who are chronically depressed and suicidal will come to the place where they know how they will end their pain, and it involves dying by suicide. Once they reach that point, their mood seems to lift and lighten. People notice that they seem to be happier or more at peace, but the only reason is that they know their pain will soon be ending. Sadly, just days before Haden's death, he had come to our house and spent some quality time individually with my husband, me, and his little brother. We all noticed he just seemed happier. It made us feel better because we thought his bout of sadness was lifting. We didn't realize we were only in the eye of the deadly storm. If you feel your loved one might be in this place, don't hesitate to bring up the topic of suicide.

---

17. National Institutes of Mental Health, "Warning Signs of Suicide," accessed August 2022, https://www.nimh.nih.gov/health/publications/warning-signs-of-suicide.

TALKING *ABOUT* SUICIDE HELPS PREVENT SUICIDE

While your loved one's talking about suicide is one of the warning signs to be aware of, avoiding the discussion can contribute to the downward spiral. There is a common myth out there that if we talk about suicide with someone who is experiencing depression, it may give them the idea, or it will cause someone who is already suicidal to go over the edge. The opposite is actually true. Many of the most successful prevention methods include directly asking if someone has plans to die by suicide. If you can, talk to a professional first. You can immediately call the 9-8-8 hotline to connect with someone who can help you know how to handle the particulars of your situation.

Some questions you might consider using when talking with someone whom you worry might be suicidal are:

- Have you been having suicidal thoughts?
- Are you thinking of killing yourself?
- Sometimes, people who are going through what you are going through think about suicide. Are you thinking of suicide?[18]

It is important to note that the tone in which you ask and the body language you use do matter. You don't want to ask in a way that conveys that you can't handle the truth or that you will shame them if the answer is yes,[19] and you must take them seriously. Please understand that if anyone ever voices that they have thoughts of taking their own life, the words need to be treated in the same way we are taught to treat a gun—as if it *is* loaded. Why do we always treat a gun as if it is loaded? Because getting it wrong could mean the end of or permanent harm to someone's life. In the same way, suicidal words are not just words; they are potentially deadly. If someone talks of suicide, *always* treat them as if they mean what they say—with compassion and positive, immediate action (see the list of action steps at the end of this

---

18. Cobain and Larch, *Dying to Be Free*, 83.
19. Ibid.

chapter). Take some form of action, no matter what they promise you, even if they seem to be joking. Koenig and Biebel share a powerful perspective in *New Light on Depression* on why to take these words seriously, and they give a few words you can say in this situation: "There are a few things in life that cannot be ignored, even if they are said jokingly. Suicide is at the top of this list because it is one thing that, if successful, cannot be undone."[20] If a person has indicated they are going to take their own life, talking, listening, reasoning, advising, and trying to restore hope aren't enough. You must also seek professional help for them.

And don't *ever* assume someone is "only wanting attention" when they bring up suicide, express suicidal ideations, or act out in self-harm, no matter how many times they have done it before. This can prove deadly. Instead, address those cries for help immediately. At the very least, call the 9-8-8 suicide hotline and speak with a counselor about what's happening with your friend or loved one. If they are crying out for help, there is still hope. Yet, if they see those cries fall on deaf ears, that last sliver of hope may disappear for them, and that's when they see no other way out.

THERE *IS* HOPE!

Suicide is preventable, and there are actions, medications, and procedures that can help stop these tragedies from happening. The first obstacles to overcome are your pride or stigmas—the fear of embarrassment, or fear of what others will think. Don't let that stop you from taking any action needed. [21] It should go without saying that your loved one's life is more important than others' opinions or even your own fears.[22] Always trust your gut and err on the side of caution in dealing with anyone whom you worry may have mood disorders or

---

20. David B. Biebel and Harold G. Koenig, *New Light on Depression: Help, Hope, and Answers for the Depressed and Those Who Love Them* (Grand Rapids, MI; Zondervan, 2003), 239.
21. SuicideLine Victoria, "Overcoming the Stigma about Suicide," accessed September 2023, https://suicideline.org.au/mental-health/overcoming-the-stigma-about-suicide/.
22. Cox and Arrington, *Aftershock*, 48.

mental health issues. Allow your loved one to try any therapy they are willing to pursue: talk therapy, prescription or homeopathic medication, nutritional supplements, prayer and spiritual deliverance, EMDR (Eye Movement Desensitization and Reprocessing) therapy, and/or electroshock treatment, among others.

In addition to medical treatment, help your loved one find hope in God. When a person is clinging to even a small thread of hope, it can hold them back from the edge. Mental health professionals agree it's often when the pain feels unending and the hope of healing seems completely gone that suicide becomes a tragic possibility. As mentioned previously, it is important to combat depression and suicidal thoughts from every front possible, and that includes someone's spiritual life. Even if you don't believe in a living relationship with God, you can't ignore the data that shows giving attention to one's spiritual life has brought hope to countless people. Often, suicidal individuals are too lost in their hopelessness to even think outside of themselves. Encourage them to pray, help them go to church and connect with brothers and sisters in Christ, offer to read the Bible with them—anything that will bring them in contact with our living hope, Jesus Christ. Spiritual hope is a supernatural empowerment given by God that can help us walk through anything in this life. If we can help those suffering from depression and suicidal tendencies touch that hope, it will give them a light in that dark place in which they have found themselves.

However, while we can all *help* to prevent suicide, it's important to know that we can *only* be there for support, not to try to *fix* this health issue for anyone. The most important thing in preventing a loved one's death by suicide is to take immediate action. As you have learned in this chapter, the following steps can help save their life.

IMMEDIATE ACTION STEPS

- If you are not with the person, call the National Suicide Prevention Lifeline at 1-800-273-TALK (8255) or dial 9-8-8. The 9-8-8 lifeline allows text and chat access to trained crisis counselors. Calling the lifeline will help you know if you or someone you love is at risk and what can be done.

- If you are with the person, let them know that suicide is not the only option out of their pain. Affirm that they are not weak, but they may be sick and need some support for healing. Call the 9-8-8 hotline while you are right there with them and support them while they talk to a professional.
- Stay with them. *Do not* leave them alone. It is critical that suicidal people are never alone.
- Remove all access to firearms, alcohol, drugs (prescription or otherwise), or sharp objects that could be used in a suicide attempt.
- Take the person to an emergency room or seek help from a medical or mental health professional.[23]

ONGOING ACTION STEPS

- Pray Scriptures over them daily. Some great Scriptures to pray are Romans 15:13, Ephesians 1:16-20, and Ephesians 3:16-19.
- Please make contact with them every day, preferably in person, and listen to their struggles, hopes, and dreams. Take the time to let them know they are not alone, that you care about them, and that they are valued and respected.
- Research local options for healthcare, including local naturopathic doctors and other alternative medicines like chiropractic and acupuncture, as well as mainstream medical options such as medical doctors who can prescribe pharmaceuticals, including antidepressants. Help them schedule an appointment, and then assist them in attending the appointment.
- Research local therapists with a good reputation for biblical

23. National Institute of Mental Health, "5 Actions Steps to Help Someone Having Thoughts of Suicide," accessed September 2023,www.nimh.nig.gov/health/publications/5-action-steps-to-help-someone-having-thoughts-of-suicide.

counseling in God's grace and love, and who have confirmed success stories. (One free resource recommended by a woman I interviewed who recovered from depression and suicidal ideation is *God's ER*, located in Tulsa, Oklahoma. You can access their self-ministry online at https://www. godser.us/ministry-overview/self-ministry/.)

- Invite them to attend church with you, and offer to pick them up. If your church has a local GriefShare, Celebrate Recovery, or similarly therapeutic group, give them the information for it and offer to join it with them. [24]

CHALLENGING THE DARKNESS: A PRAYER FOR THE FIGHT

Beth Ann Baus, with the Association of Certified Biblical Counselors, shared an important insight regarding praying when you're in the thick of suicidal ideation. She shares how it is often hardest to pray when you are consumed with suicidal thoughts. She says, "It's a good idea to plan ahead. Write a prayer when you're able to express your pain and thought process, then you'll have it ready to read the next time the suicidal thoughts come."[25] The following is just one example of a prayer you can pray.

Dear God,

Help me! You said, 'Greater is He who is in me than he who is in the world.' Your light is greater than this darkness. I choose You. My life belongs to You. It is not mine. But this pain seems more than unbearable. God of hope, help me to believe You, and fill me with all joy and peace in believing so that I can abound with hope by the power of Your Holy Spirit.

Help me believe that You are with me and I am not alone. Help me believe that You see me when I feel invisible. Help me remember that I am of infinite

24. God's ER, "Self Ministry," accessed September 2023, https://www.godser.us/ministry-overview/self-ministry/.
25. Beth Ann Baus, "A Prayer for Fighting Suicidal Thoughts," Crosswalk.com, September 5, 2024, https://www.crosswalk.com/faith/prayer/a-prayer-for-fighting-suicidal-thoughts.html.

worth, and You have proven that by purchasing my life with the highest price of Heaven —the life of Your Son, Jesus Christ. Renew my hope. Give me a vision of the future. Please show me how to defeat this enemy that wants to take my life. Help me to receive Your forgiveness fully.

Help me to understand that my slate is clean and that shame, condemnation, and self-loathing are liars. I reject them in the name of Jesus. Show me all the lies my heart has accepted that agree with this torment, and help me to believe the truth that will set me free. You said my life matters and that I have purpose and value. I choose to agree with You. My life DOES matter. I DO have a purpose, and it is to find victory and freedom from this torment in the land of the living. My life IS valuable. I belong to You. And I choose to let You love me and help me see the truth.

In Jesus's precious name, amen.

CHAPTER 10

BECOMING A SUICIDE SURVIVOR: YOU CAN SURVIVE—AND YOU WILL

One thing I want to say to survivors is: You were enough.
—Forever19

Just weeks after my son's passing, I wasn't sleeping well at night, so mid-morning, I went upstairs to lie in the collage of beds we had positioned side by side on the floor as an initial survival tactic. I slept for about an hour, and just as I was starting to stir, I saw someone standing off to the side as if waiting for me to wake up.

This individual stood with their weight shifted to one leg and their hands tucked into their front pockets. I couldn't make out who it was, but then they came and knelt beside me. I propped myself up on my elbows, squinting and narrowing my eyes, struggling to make out what the person was doing. I realized they were tracing something in the air with their pointer finger.

Confused, I squinted harder and shook my head, trying to make it out. Suddenly, I realized what they were drawing in the air was the infinity sign.

The symbol hovered in my mind like a word on the tip of the tongue—just out of reach. Then I became fully awake. The person was gone. Still resting on my elbows, I lay frozen, holding my breath, not wanting to interrupt this surreal moment. My mouth fell open as my head drew back in awe, and I, in shock, sucked in a deep breath. I thought to myself, *That was Haden! But what does that sign mean? Was he trying to tell me something?* My brow furrowed as I racked my brain. I thought to myself, '*Oh, that's the infinity sign!' It means? Infinite? Infinity? Infinite... love?' Was he letting me know that wherever he was, he was receiving infinite love and that he loved us infinitely?*

I thought back to when I'd first seen him standing off to the side. I wasn't ever able to make out who it was, but then I remembered how he was standing—his weight shifted to one leg, and his hands were in his pockets. It was just like Haden always used to stand.

Before this experience, I had never given much thought to the infinity sign. I barely even knew what it meant. However, it has now become so special to me. Every time I see the sign, I think of my son. Only later did I learn that the infinity symbol also represents eternity.

Often, when we lose someone close to us, we experience special moments of connection with them after they pass, whether it be in a dream, a vision, or another form. Some call these "Whispers from Heaven" or "God Winks," but I'd prefer to coin the phrase "Infinite Connections." Now, understand, I'm not here to tell you whether those moments are real or not. I'm not here to tell whether they are something from God or not. And I'm not about to say to you, as some wiseacre would, if you have something like this happen, that it's just a hallucination. If we believe in a supernatural God that can speak to us through dreams, visions, and miracles, why wouldn't we have faith that He can supernaturally bring us comfort during some of the worst trials of our lives? I don't care if anyone else in the world believes this connection moment I had with my son. No one else *need* believe it, but I will say it has brought me great comfort, and I will treasure it *forever*. In fact, I think it has helped me survive this tragedy. This Infinite Connection felt like a reassurance that God and my son were giving to me, letting me know that my son was in eternity and he was being infinitely loved, that he was okay, and that our family would find peace, too.

Regardless of whether you have had a special connection moment like this, I want you to realize that we *all* share a special connection with our lost loved ones who have passed in Christ. Unlike some, I never really felt closer to my son at the graveside. The only two places I really felt closer to my son were when I looked at pictures or when I worshiped. I didn't quite understand why I felt closer to him when I was worshiping God, until I came across Hebrews 12:23. Paraphrasing this Scripture, we see that when Christians (on earth) come together to worship, they come not only into the presence of God in Heaven, but also into the presence of the spirits of the redeemed in Heaven who have now been made perfect. Who are the spirits of the redeemed? None other than *our* loved ones who believed in Jesus but went on to Heaven before us. I believe one of those spirits of the redeemed is my son, Haden. One of those spirits of the redeemed may very well be *your* lost loved one. And what does the rest of the verse say? They have "now been made perfect." Hallelujah. No more sickness, disease, crying, confusion, or pain. They are perfect in mind, body, and soul— whole in Christ.

Throughout this book, I've used the term *suicide griever* to speak of those of us who have lost a loved one to suicide. Yet there was a point when I knew I was no longer a suicide griever, but I had become *a suicide survivor*—a person who had walked through the grief of losing a loved one by suicide and came out the other side a survivor. My prayer is that you find that place, as well. It may take years, but if you draw near to God and implement what you have found in these pages, I trust you will find your way to *suicide survivor*! Dear friend, you are stronger than you know. You can survive, and you will!

I pray that, as a result of reading this book, you have felt heard, understood, and seen, and, in turn, have come to realize that *you are not alone*. I trust you have seen what a shared human experience traumatic grief is. What a shared human experience suicide loss is. And I'm confident you have found survival tactics to help you traverse your grief.

I pray you see our Creator as the greatest Source for the recon- struction of your life after such a devastating loss and as the best avenue to find true repair for your heart, mind, and soul.

I pray a spiritual transformation has begun in your life. A transfor-

mation from grief, bitterness, anger, and confusion to a place of healing, forgiveness, peace, and hope. I pray you understand that for this
transformation of your faith to occur, it may take doing some things
you don't necessarily want to do. Drawing near to God may not be the
easiest thing right now, but I can *assure* you it is the best avenue to
healing and wholeness. And most importantly, regarding your faith, I
pray you come to see, just as I did, the *depth* of God's love not only for
you but also for your lost loved one.

One of the best truths I found on my healing journey in regard to
suffering came from a small book written in the early 1900s by evange-
list and author Henry Frost. Frost made various observations about
those who prayed for healing. One important observation he noted
was "the attitude of those who prayed was not that of claiming healing,
as if a universal right had been established by the atoning work of
Christ, but rather that of seeking God's will in the case." This means
those who prayed exercised their faith not in positive assurance that
"one" specific outcome would happen, but they prayed for God's will.
Further, he noted that their positive assurance was *primarily* in the
"power, love, and wisdom of God." When I read that, I realized we
shouldn't necessarily have faith in *this* specific thing or *that* specific
thing to happen, but we should have faith that God will be by our side
regardless of the situation. Ultimately, we should have faith in the
"power, love, and wisdom of God." So, if we have faith in Him, walk
according to His ways, and trust that His ways are good, we can be
assured that leaving the results of *everything* in God's hands is our best
bet in this life and the next. Although it seems impossible, we must
look at our trials and loss in the same way. God allowed it, and we
must, by faith, believe in the power, love, and wisdom of God.

Friend, I pray that you not only find healing in your grief but that
you see the good that God is bringing about from this pain. I pray that
you take everything that Satan meant for your destruction and turn it
for good. That you create purpose from your pain so that it doesn't just
end in pain. That you, in turn, when the time is right, will learn to
comfort others with the same comfort you have received. I pray that
you find a deeper faith and a stronger hope than you've ever known

before. I pray that God becomes the strength of your heart. I pray I have helped to build your faith in our Father.

Furthermore, I hope you have learned how important it is to process your emotions, especially during grief, and if you don't, that it can genuinely hurt your health mentally and physically. Remember, those emotions must come up and out to be healed. They can't be swept under the rug, potentially causing you to become stuck in grief or mental breakdown. Remember, as God's Word says, we must take every thought captive to make it obedient to Christ (2 Corinthians 10:3–5 NKJV).

And, let me reiterate the quote at the beginning of this chapter because it's so important to hear. Dear friend,

You...

were...

enough!

You brought what you needed to the relationship you shared with your lost loved one. You brought love, beautiful qualities, and your presence. Your love, support, and efforts were valued. They weren't overlooked or underappreciated. You didn't fall short! I understand how heavy your heart can feel, to fear or worry that your departed one didn't feel loved, or perhaps worse, that the love you shared wasn't enough to save them. Let me share some words from a young man who knows both sides of the aisle. He not only attempted to take his own life, but later lost one of his best friends to suicide. He, too, spoke about this worry we often have, "that our love wasn't enough to make them stay," yet he shares these comforting words: "But, I can tell you what your love did do, if that helps: It made their time here on earth so much more meaningful. I can also promise you it sustained them in many, *many* dark moments that they never told you about."[1]

I've come to believe that our loved one's suicide says nothing about the degree, strength, or quality of our love for them, nor of their love

---

1. Sam Finch, "5 Things Suicide Loss Survivors Should Know," Healthline, December 21, 2019, https://www.healthline.com/health/mental-health/losing-someone-to-suicide.

for us. If they had died of any other illness, would we question whether they felt loved or not? Likely not. A lack of love was not the *cause* of their pain, but rather the love we shared might have been the only light that stayed with them in some of their darkest moments.

And of great importance, I pray you know your loved one's passing is *not your fault*! You did the best you could mentally, physically, spiritually, and relationally. I pray you have learned how to throw off false guilt and deal with true guilt. And if you battle guilt, remember, it may take time and upwards of one thousand rounds, but you can chip away at that boulder of guilt until it is gone. Fight using Scripture like Romans 8:1: "So now there is no condemnation for those who belong to Christ Jesus."

Additionally, I hope I have encouraged you to embrace a new perspective regarding mental health issues and suicide—one that promotes understanding and empathy and challenges the stigmas surrounding these issues. But my greatest hope and prayer, aside from helping you to traverse suicide grief, is that I have created an awareness that prevents even *one* person from finding this same tragic fate. If you are someone who suffers from depression or suicidal thoughts, I pray I have helped you see yourself better. I hope I have helped you see that you are *not* weak; it is *not* personal failure, but rather that you are quite likely suffering from an illness that needs medical attention. Or maybe it's simply in sharing what you have learned, which finds its way into someone's heart and mind, helping them realize they aren't a failure but instead may be dealing with an illness that needs medical attention.

Of utmost importance, I earnestly pray, that you have come to understand better where your loved one likely was on that fateful day. I pray you have learned how your loved one, in all likelihood, was ill. They didn't *choose* to leave you, but more likely, they honestly thought that what they were doing was best for everyone. Of course, we know that isn't true in the least, but I hope you can more clearly see this is likely what their ill mind, in its illness, believed. I'm positive my son loved me just as much as I am sure your loved one loved and cared for you so deeply.

God has comforted me in my trial, and I pray that I have been able to pass on that comfort to you, my friend. I know surviving the loss of someone to suicide seems so impossible, but I pray that as a result of reading this book, you can indeed see light at the end of your tunnel. I pray you have found that you can move forward and lead a good life despite the tragedy you have had to endure. It may take quite some time before you are there, but if you keep moving forward, allowing yourself to grieve and process your emotions, and just keep walking toward God, asking Him about anything and everything, you will find healing and restoration. I'm confident of that. I pray you not only find that you can live, but that you find a desire to live life to the fullest.

As mental health advocate Sam Finch once wrote in an article for *Healthline*: "You're part of the legacy your loved one left behind. And every moment you choose to live fully and love deeply, you bring a beautiful part of them back to life. Fight for your own life the way you so desperately wish you could've fought for theirs. You are just as worthy. I promise you."[2]

Although you've made it to the end of this book, your journey through this traumatic grief may very well take years; don't allow people to rush you through your grief. Take the time you need. I would encourage you, if you haven't already, to find a GriefShare program near you and potentially a suicide loss support group, either online or in person. God created us for community, and the need for that is never more evident than during loss or trial. At this time, go back through the book to review any areas needed or any areas that you may have completely skipped because they were just too hard. You need to not only understand your grief and overcome any crisis in your faith, but a greater peace will come as you better understand death by suicide and any mental illness that may have affected your loved one.

Looking forward, another thing that I did and would suggest is to learn all you can about Heaven; it will bring you great comfort knowing what your loved one may be experiencing now. And as you learn about our eternal hope, you will surely not grieve like those who have no hope.

I can't recommend *In Light of Eternity* by Randy Alcorn enough.

---

2. Finch, "5 Things Suicide Loss Survivors Should Know."

This is an easy read that brought me so much peace, understanding, and, dare I say, joy. I pray you, too, can find this peace and joy in regards to eternity. Friend, I was in a similar place as you, and these are the steps that helped me to find hope and joy in life again. I know you can find it, too.

There is something about having lived through the worst imaginable and surviving that strengthens your faith and character. There is something about realizing your frailty that helps you recognize your need and dependence on God. There is something about living through a situation with absolutely no control that helps you want to abide by the One who has complete control. There is something about suffering that helps us learn compassion for others.

There is something about being comforted that helps us realize we are better equipped to comfort others. There is something about experiencing death so closely that makes our focus turn more to our eternal life rather than this temporal one. There is *something* at work in God's plan. And when we align our lives with His plan, we have the best Life Author we could ever hope to have.

Dear Lord,

Just as You tell us in Your Word that You and the heroes of the faith watch as we take our turn at this race, Lord, help me to be made strong in my weakness, so that I may, by faith, finish the race set before me. Help me, Lord, to realize that following You isn't just about living a blessed life, but it's about picking up our cross, no matter how heavy it is, and carrying it to the end of the line. And just as the promise of the future hope and joy abundant in Heaven gave You the strength to suffer, help me to take confidence in that same future hope and joy so I can be made strong enough to survive my trials. Help me to heal, to move forward, to find joy, to find peace, and to find comfort in knowing that You are by my side every step of the way. Thank You for the amazing eternity you have planned for me and my loved ones.

In Jesus's name, amen.

ACKNOWLEDGMENTS

To my immediate family,

Thank you for joining me in doing the important work to heal from our loss. Thank you for strengthening me when I was weak and for allowing me to grieve when and how I needed to. It was having each of you that gave me inspiration to live and heal. I'm especially grateful for your encouragement in writing this book, which we believe has been an assignment from God. By faith, we trust it has the power to raise awareness of this devastating illness, share the hope and healing we have found, and ultimately honor the memory of our son and brother. Thank you for loving me so well and believing in me so much. Robert, Brittany, and Dylan, you are my world.

I love you all wholeheartedly,
    Victoria

~

To those who encouraged me along the way,

I would be remiss not to thank our family and friends who walked with us along the way, not only through this tragedy but through the writing of this book. Thank you for your encouragement and love.

And a special thank you to Maria Gardner, our GriefShare leader. You are an amazing woman of God, and I'm so thankful that He blessed our family not only with your guidance and counsel but also with your friendship. Thank you for helping to guide me back to our Heavenly Father.

Thank you, Rachel Bradley, for being a fantastic book coach who helped me wade through the good, the bad, and the ugly to decipher the beneficial, as well as for encouraging me along the way and enduring all my author meltdowns. You have been a true blessing.

And foremost, I want to thank the best Counselor there is. Thank You, Holy Spirit. Thank You for leading me back to God, comforting me and my family, opening God's Word like never before, and introducing me to a God I never knew, but for whom I now have the highest respect.

With gratitude and love,
    Victoria Myers

Appendix A

Spouse and Sibling Matters in Grief

While all our stories are different and some of us have lost a friend, cousin, or spouse to suicide, I would like to briefly address a few family relationship dynamics and types of suicide loss that we've personally experienced. If you've lost a sibling or a child to suicide, this section is especially for you.

After our loss, I knew it was important to draw our family together. One thing that brought comfort in the first few weeks after the traumatic loss of our son was to bring all our mattresses together, and we all slept in the same room. I knew that if my kids had the same fears seething through them that I had, they needed as much comforting as possible. I believe this co-sleeping helped us all. When any of us awoke at night in fear, we could see the rest of our family right beside us, and this brought such comfort.

In those first weeks, we also came together each night right before bed. We talked and read from a book about Heaven, sharing anything we were learning from books or counseling sessions with each other. We spent time in prayer, cried together, and asked each other questions or shared how we were feeling. I wanted to reassure each of my children that their grief was normal and to let them know that the lines of communication were open.

HOW SIBLINGS MAY EXPERIENCE UNIQUE TRIALS IN LOSS

Siblings who have lost a loved one often grieve in similar and very different ways than their parents do; this was certainly true in our experience. Book after book pointed this out, but this in no way means the siblings hurt any less than the parents. In fact, siblings feel grief deeply and experience many of the same emotions their parents are going through. They, too, experience shock and disbelief. They experience fear and frequently wonder if something will happen to another family member or themselves. Some young people feel guilt for still being alive when their sibling isn't or guilt that they said or did something that might have hurt their sibling. They may feel anger or sadness for all the future times or events their sibling will miss. They might experience physical ailments, like adults, and may even experience a type of depression because of their grief. One helpful book on relationships during grief and how children cope with their grief was *Surviving the Loss of a Child* by Elizabeth B. Brown. Mrs. Brown shared that young people often don't show their grief, or at times, they seem to have delayed grief. In my estimation, there may be many reasons for this, one being that they likely *never* saw their parents in such intense pain before, and the last thing they would want to do is include their grief on top of that. So, they may often tuck their grief away. However, grief doesn't just go away, and it will likely resurface at some point in the future, in one way or another. They need to be reassured that it is okay and necessary to grieve.

To my disappointment, my daughter shared that there were a few individuals who told her she needed "to be strong for her parents." I assured her she didn't, and that she had every right to release her grief as well as any of us. In fact, she was the one who had found her brother, so she likely had even more trauma to traverse than we did. It took her seven months to overcome her fear of walking through a closed door, fearing what she might find on the other side. She did undergo EMDR (Eye Movement Desensitization and Reprocessing) therapy, which she believed truly helped her. EMDR helps to reduce symptoms of trauma by changing how your memories are stored in your brain.

It's important to know that often, children in the family feel like no one cares about their grief. My children noticed that so many people seemed to ask how their parents were doing, but then they never seemed to ask how *they* were doing. In the loss of a child, the parents are focused on, almost to an extreme, which leaves the other siblings feeling even more lost and less cared for than ever. We noticed this personally, as well.

Another common occurrence in grief for siblings is the disproportionate amount of admiration often shown by parents for the deceased child. Oftentimes, with the loss of a loved one, our hearts are so hurt by losing them that any character flaws or wrongs they ever did are thrown out the window, and sometimes, even worse, parents often seem almost to glorify the lost child. Sadly, this may very well hurt the siblings. Making them feel less valued. We could see the potential for this in our family, as well, so we reassured our other kids not only about how amazing they were but that they were just as important, and we would be just as sad if we had lost one of them.

SPOUSES MAY GRIEVE DIFFERENTLY, AND THAT'S OKAY

I was shocked by how differently our whole family grieved, especially the significant differences between my husband and me. My husband constantly commented that he felt like this pain had no expiration date, and he wanted it to end soon. I, on the other hand, assumed it would take years, if not a lifetime, to walk through this grief.

In the first few weeks following the loss of our son, I wasn't sure our marriage would survive. One day, I was so overcome with this possibility that I started having anxiety attacks. I had read some books that gave staggering and confusing statistics for divorce. Some said up to 90 percent of parents' divorce after the loss of a child to suicide. Not that I was looking for the statistic to tell me the strength of my marriage, but it just added to my confusion and concern. However, the more I learned about how differently spouses may grieve over the loss of a child, the more at ease I became.

One of the most challenging parts for my husband and me was how confused we were by each other's grief. Robert and I grieved so differently, and I remember thinking, *How can we both be the parents of the same boy, and both grieve and think so differently about all of this?*

He buried himself in work, and I buried myself in the hope of healing. He claimed I moped all day, and I claimed he didn't process his grief enough. Then it felt like we didn't even match the differences some of the books touted. Some books said women usually liked to talk about their loss, but men didn't. For us, it was the opposite. I didn't like talking about it with him because I secretly worried that if he saw how deep my grief truly was, it would make *his* grief worse and cause him to plummet even deeper into depression. I also knew he would likely try to "fix" me and my grief, and I knew he couldn't do that, no matter how badly he might want to.

Another notable difference was dealing with ordering a gravestone. I felt this was one of the last meaningful things I could do for my son; my husband wanted nothing to do with it. I liked to look at pictures of our son. He couldn't stand it. I wanted just to be held, and that seemed oblivious to him. He, on the other hand, wanted to make love, but I couldn't bring myself to even think of it. He was ready to go back to church. I wasn't. He wanted to talk with others about our loss. I didn't want to talk to anyone about it. Luckily, in our counseling and reading, we found out we both needed just to step back and allow each other the space to grieve in our own ways. If we tried to force our grief practices on each other, it would just cause even more hurt, anger, and confusion.

Another example of our processing grief so differently happened when I took the large canvas pictures of our son from the funeral, and I placed them on the wall and mantel. One day, when I got home, one of them was behind the couch. I asked my husband what happened, and he said he couldn't stand looking at them. This scared me. I thought, *Does he want to forget our son altogether? However,* when I spoke with our counselor about it, she explained that husbands and wives typically grieve quite differently. She suggested I be sensitive to everyone at this time and that I might consider taking down the pictures and putting them up in rooms my husband didn't frequent. I waited several months, then slowly added them back one by one. My husband said this helped him. It wasn't that he wanted to forget our son, but the constant face-to-face was too much for him to bear at the time. It's okay to grieve differently from others in your family.

In losing a child to suicide, there was great potential for us to blame each other for our son's death, and at different points, we both did blame each other to some degree. Thankfully, we both worked through this in our counseling sessions and our time with God.

I want to reiterate that getting outside help is so crucial during traumatic grief because it can help not only in dealing with the traumatic grief but also in dealing with your relationships during this time. I feel that if we had not been in counseling and continuously studying to understand this type of grief, our marriage might not have survived. Thankfully, the information we acquired helped us see that we would grieve quite differently. This knowledge also helped us be able to communicate with each other better instead of being alienated by our grief differences.

I believe the main characteristics that saved our marriage were threefold: our solid commitment to each other, our determination to heal for the rest of our family, and, foremost, our drawing back to God. After a life has been demolished by traumatic loss, we need to muster the strength to fight for our relationships because grief may have reorganized or confused them.

God's Word says that when two are laboring together, they have a greater return for their labor (Ecclesiastes 4:9 NKJV). I'd say this applies even if what they are laboring in is grief. It was good to see how, when I was weaker, Robert was there for me, and he was stronger. And then, if he was feeling weak, I could be strong for him. Above all things, remember to have a lot of grace with your spouse at this time. You both will likely need it like never before.

While this appendix focuses on specific relationships in grief my family has experienced, I encourage you to find information that addresses your specific relationship needs or dynamics. The dynamics in every relationship are different and, as we've seen, can be pretty confusing during times of grief.

Appendix B

Depression Self-Check

The World Health Organization provides a Depression Self-Assessment Tool, which is an online assessment you can take. You can find it at: https://worldhealthorg.shinyapps.io/steps_depression_tool/

Important Note: Different types of depression may have symptoms or duration of symptoms that differ. Also, while there is a difference between major depression and depression you may experience during grief, they do share some of the same symptoms. It is best to speak with a healthcare provider to distinguish between depression that may be experienced during grief and major depression.

Appendix C
Recommended Resources by Topic

Note: These are ordered in each section according to which resource I felt was most helpful.

Author's Website

www.AuthorVictoriaMyers.com

Dealing with Grief in General

- *Teen Grief: Caring for the Teenage Grieving Heart* by Gary Roe (actually suitable for any age)
- GriefShare is a free support group that helps you move through the process of grief (griefshare.org)
- *You Are the Mother of All Mothers: A Message of Hope for the Grieving Heart* by Angela Miller (specifically for grieving mothers)
- *Surviving the Loss of a Child: Support for Grieving Parents* by Elizabeth B. Brown
- *Grieving God's Way: The Path to Lasting Hope and Healing* by Margaret Brownley (a 90-day devotional)

- *Jonathan, You Left Too Soon* by David B. Biebel
- *Healing after Loss: Daily Meditations for Working through Grief* by Martha W. Hickman
- Journal prompts, podcast episodes, and other resources from Kari Bartkus, a spiritual director for those who have experienced grief or trauma (lovedoesthat.org)

DEALING WITH SUICIDE GRIEF AND KNOWLEDGE OF SUICIDE

- *Grieving a Suicide: A Loved One's Search for Comfort, Answers, and Hope* by Albert Y. Hsu (if you can only order one book on my resource page, this should be it!)
- *Finding Your Way after the Suicide of Someone You Love* by David B. Biebel, DMin, and Suzanne L. Foster, MA
- American Association of Suicidology's *SOS Handbook for Survivors of Suicide* by Jeffrey Jackson
- *Aftershock Help, Hope, and Healing in the Wake of Suicide* by David Cox and Candy Arrington
- *Suicide Survivors: A Guide for Those Left Behind* by Adina Wrobleski
- *Dying to Be Free: A Healing Guide for Families after a Suicide* by Beverly Cobain and Jean Larch

DEALING WITH GOD, FAITH QUESTIONS, SUFFERING, AND EMOTIONAL TRAUMA

- *If God Is So Good, Why Do I Hurt So Bad?* by David B. Biebel, DMin
- *A Place of Healing: Wrestling with the Mysteries of Suffering, Pain, and God's Sovereignty* by Joni Eareckson Tada
- *Hearing Jesus Speak into Your Sorrow* by Nancy Guthrie
- *The Pause App* is a free app by John Eldridge that is based on some of his books. This app helps foster your connection with God and includes such applications as meditations, journaling, prayer, etc.).

- *A Step Further* by Joni Eareckson Tada and Steve Estes
- *If God Is Good: Faith in the Midst of Suffering and Evil* by Randy Alcorn

UNDERSTANDING SUICIDE OR MENTAL ILLNESS

- *Bruised and Wounded: Struggling to Understand Suicide* by Ronald Holheiser
- *Troubled Minds: Mental Illness and the Church's Mission* by Amy Simpson, foreword by Marshall Shelley
- *Myths about Suicide* by Thomas Joiner
- *Night Falls Fast* by Kay Redfield Jamison

UNDERSTANDING DEPRESSION (NOT NECESSARILY CONCERNING GRIEF)

- *New Light on Depression: Help, Hope, and Answers for the Depressed and Those Who Love Them* by David B. Biebel, DMin. and Harold G. Koenig, MD
- *What to Do When Someone You Love Is Depressed: A Practical, Compassionate, and Helpful Guide* by Mitch Golant, PhD, and Susan K. Golant

UNDERSTANDING MORE ABOUT HEAVEN

- *In Light of Eternity: Perspectives on Heaven* by Randy Alcorn (an easy read that gets straight to the point)
- *Imagine Heaven: Near-Death Experiences, God's Promises, and the Exhilarating Future That Awaits You* by John Burke

OTHER AVENUES FOR MENTAL HEALTH SUPPORT

Online Talk Therapy: There are many different companies, but I suggest that you see a Christian counselor. Online therapy eliminates the need to travel for people with mobility issues, with time constraints, or without close access to care. It also helps individuals to feel more comfortable talking with someone from the comfort of their own home, which may allow the sessions to be more successful. Some even offer text or chat therapy.

Mission15four.org: Recognizing peer support as one of the major components in addressing mental health issues, Nick Nelson's nonprofit provides this vital resource. Born out of a passion for making sure no one battles alone, his organization fosters community by helping individuals to feel seen, heard, and more connected. He offers one-on-one guidance to men who are not able to pursue professional counseling. (Nick Nelson, Founder, Mission15four.org)

About the Author

Victoria Myers is an author and writer whose passion is to encourage others through faith, honesty, and hope in the midst of life's deepest losses. After experiencing the devastating loss of her son, she began writing as both a personal lifeline and a way to walk alongside others facing grief.

Today, Victoria facilitates grief support groups and creates resources to remind others they are not alone. Through her book, blog, and newsletter, she shares encouragement, reflections, and practical hope for those navigating loss.

You can connect with Victoria and explore additional resources at www.authorvictoriamyers.com, or simply scan the QR code below to go directly to her website.

www.ingramcontent.com/pod-product-compliance
Lightning Source LLC
Chambersburg PA
CBHW030828090426
42737CB00009B/920